Drumming from Within

Drumming from Within

Tales of Hope and Faith
from Canada's North

Archbishop Sylvain Lavoie OMI

NOVALIS

© 2009 Novalis Publishing Inc.

Cover design: Blair Turner
Cover artwork: *The Sacred Journey* 2008, painted by Fr. Robert Laroche OMI
Layout: Audrey Wells

Published by Novalis

Publishing Office
10 Lower Spadina Avenue, Suite 400
Toronto, Ontario, Canada
M5V 2Z2

Head Office
4475 Frontenac Street
Montréal, Québec, Canada
H2H 2S2

www.novalis.ca

Library and Archives Canada Cataloguing in Publication

Lavoie, Sylvain, 1947-
        Drumming from within : tales of hope and faith from Canada's North /
Sylvain Lavoie.

ISBN 978-2-89646-151-6

        1. Lavoie, Sylvain, 1947-. 2. Native peoples--Canada, Northern--Missions. 3. Pastoral
theology--Catholic Church. 4. Catholic Church--Missions--Canada, Northern. 5. Oblates
of Mary Immaculate--Biography. 6. Catholic Church-- Canada--Clergy--Biography. I. Title.

BX4705.L417A3 2009   271'.7602   C2009-903933-8

Printed in Canada.

The Scripture quotations contained herein are from the New Revised Standard Version of
the Bible, copyrighted 1989 by the Division of Christian Education of the National Council
of the Churches of Christ in the United States of America, and are used by permission. All
rights reserved.

We acknowledge the financial support of the Government of Canada through the Canada
Book Fund for business development activities.

5   4   3   18   17   16   15   14

Table of Contents

Acknowledgments

The day after I arrived for summer ministry in Île-à-la-Crosse, Saskatchewan, as a young scholastic brother in 1972, I set out to explore the sandy southern tip of the community that juts out into the lake. There, sheltered in the protective custody of sturdy, windblown spruce trees, was the cemetery. In the middle of it, marked out by a low chain fence, were the graves of all the Oblate priests and brothers and the religious women who had so selflessly served the people of the north in the past. I was almost overwhelmed by a sense of how much faith, love and dedicated service in this part of the vast Archdiocese of Keewatin-The Pas those dates etched in stone symbolized.

Now, as this book of stories about ministry in this same area is published decades and even a century later, I feel humbled by their silent witness. I am filled with a profound sentiment of respect and gratitude for the many veteran Oblate missionary priests and brothers who laid the foundations, such as Bishop Ovide Charlebois, Fr. Taché, Fr. Moraud and Bro. Dionne.

Thanks also to my Oblate confrères and the Grey Nuns of Montreal and Pembroke, the Sisters of Mission Service, the Sisters of St. Elizabeth, les Filles de la Providence, the Ursulines of Prelate, and the Sisters of Charity of the Immaculate Conception, who served so generously and provided solid support over those first years of my ministry in the Archdiocese of Keewatin-The Pas. I am also grateful for my association with the Presentation of Mary sisters, with whom I ministered as part of a team for six years in the adjoining diocese of Prince Albert. That gratitude now extends to the Adrian Dominican sisters from the United States, who have recently come to minister in our archdiocese.

A special word of thanks to the late Archbishop Paul Dumouchel OMI, who trusted us so completely as young priests, and Archbishop Emeritus Peter Sutton OMI, whose understanding, sensitivity to the needs of the people, unflagging encouragement and personal support led to the formation of the Keewatin Renewal Team and a priceless archdiocesan experience from 1987 to 1990.

I also owe a debt of gratitude to Bishop Emeritus Blaise Morand, whose support and encouragement I could always count on during the almost twelve years that I spent ministering in the diocese of Prince Albert. It was fitting that he was one of the consecrators at my episcopal ordination in The Pas on August 29, 2005.

Another person I want to thank is Sr. Mary Kastens OP, the Director of Religious Education for our archdiocese. Her generous willingness to proofread the text with a keen critical eye and her learned suggestions were a real gift to me in preparing this manuscript for publication.

Even though she belongs to the Carrier First Nation, I want to say a very sincere thank you or, in Cree, *ki nanâskomitin*, to Dr. Maggie Hodgson. "Mags," as she calls herself, was the director of Nechi Institute and Poundmaker's Lodge, a renowned addictions treatment and training centre in St. Albert, Alberta. I treasure her wisdom as an elder, her zest for life as a human being and her ability to affirm and challenge as a friend. I was honoured to be co-presenter with her at a church conference in Edmonton in 2008, and now am honoured that she graciously accepted to write the foreword for this book, and wrote it in her own inimitable style.

A sincere thank you also to the staff of Novalis for agreeing to publish this book, especially editors Joe Sinasac and Anne Louise Mahoney, for their patience, dedication and improvements to the text.

Above all, thanks to the northern people of God, whose faith, love, acceptance, humour, openness, trust, affirmation and ability to challenge helped a young Oblate priest mature in faith, love and service of Jesus Christ and his Body, the Church.

Foreword

Drumming from Within is the journey of a young man seeking, exploring, risking, doubting, hoping and growing in humility while learning what God's words of love mean in his life and the lives of the people among whom he lived and ministered.

Through traditional storytelling, Archbishop Lavoie teaches about life as a priest. He explores the deepening of God's Spirit within himself and those he stands with as they take steps into finding peace. By sharing with his flock the Search for Christian Maturity weekends, Christopher Leadership Courses, Twelve Step Pilgrimages and other skills and introspective opportunities, he taught them how to fish instead of fishing for them.

Archbishop Lavoie shines a light in the shadows while taking risks by trying out new ways to open doors to freedom for himself and the people he lived with in community. He walks the road between preaching God's word and learning to see God's word in action in the empowerment taking place through the programs he initiated wherever he served.

His acceptance of love from others was an open door for him. He was able to create an environment in which community members felt safe to deal with their past hurts. His pioneer healing work made it possible for others wounded by their residential school experience to heal.

Archbishop Lavoie's life work of trusting God's grace while questioning himself exemplifies his faith and courage. We journey with him as a young Oblate missionary priest who finally becomes a man with the garments of an archbishop and a heart full of love.

He teaches about being both a learner and a teacher in his invitation to people who are thinking about service in the Church community. This book is a must read for new pastoral ministers working in the Church, as well as for all members of our Canadian society. It is the first book I have read that is written from such a unique perspective of contemporary Church life. I know many who do good work, but I have never heard of anyone taking the time to write about the stumbling, the running forward, the risking and the exploring as Archbishop Lavoie has done.

Through his eyes, heart and experience, and within the limits of his humanity, Archbishop Lavoie has come to understand and live the words of St. Eugene de Mazenod, founder of the Missionary Oblates: "Leave nothing undared."

Dr. Maggie Hodgson
Edmonton, Alberta

Introduction

"Father is here – we're going to have Church."

These words of wisdom came from the mouths of children who spoke them in their homes. For them, their home was where Church was happening, not just in the building called the "church." How healthy that is!

These words aptly describe my early experience of "Church" in northern Saskatchewan and in northern Manitoba. Church was happening everywhere and all the time. Looking back, I see that the north was a great place for a young Oblate to begin ministry.

For some years I dreamed of capturing in writing the unique flavour of ministry among the northern people. First Nations and Métis, Cree and Dené, as well as non-Aboriginal, all blend together in a portion of God's beautiful creation that makes for an experience and a lifestyle that is truly "northern."

I was raised in the heart of Plains Cree country around North Battleford, Saskatchewan, yet had little interaction with the First Nations peoples as I was growing up. We were surrounded by seven First Nations communities, yet rarely saw the people living on those "reserves," as they were called. I didn't realize it at the time, but the *pass and permit* colonial system, which controlled the lives of the First Nations peoples, was still in effect. Within this system, the people who lived on the reserves had to obtain permission from the Indian Agent to both leave the reserve to visit other communities and to sell their produce. In effect, the Indian Agent had almost total control over the lives of the people, and sometimes abused that power.

I learned much later that the land my father homesteaded was the rich farmland "between the two rivers" that was coveted by the settlers. That land was finally obtained for the settlers, through political and economic pressure tactics, from the First Nations of Thunderchild and Moosomin, who were relocated on less desirable land further north.

I still have pangs of sadness whenever I visit the location of the former hamlet of Highgate, where I went to elementary school and played as a child in what used to be the cemetery of the First Nations peoples. The bodies had been exhumed and relocated along with the people. Ironically, the one-room Whitecap Elementary School that I attended for eight years was named after the former chief of the First Nations community situated just south of Saskatoon at Dundurn, Saskatchewan.

Perhaps the invisibility of the First Nations people in their own territory as I grew up provided an underlying motive for me to write these stories. I hope, in some small way, to make more visible the richness of the First Nations and Métis peoples that I have experienced in over 30 years of ministry with and among them.

My first taste of First Nations and Métis ministry happened during my first year as a theology student at St. Charles Scholasticate, the Oblate house of formation just south of Battleford, Saskatchewan. As students, we were expected to take part in some form of ministry; I chose to join a team of Oblates and two religious women who were running *Miyo-Wîcehtowin*, a coffee house and youth club for First Nations and Métis youth.

We had weekly gatherings and occasionally meetings with the youth, during which it became obvious that most of the initiative was coming from the staff. We were "doing for them" more than "doing with."

Two events that happened during that year influenced me as a young Oblate considering First Nations ministry.

The first event involved the coffee house. We had encouraged the youth to resist asking for grants that would have political strings attached to them and to instead raise their own funds. This they did quite successfully. At Christmas, we had enough money to put on a Christmas party, which dozens of youth attended.

As this was our last gathering before we all dispersed for Christmas, we, as leaders, had decided to celebrate a Eucharist at midnight as a way to end the party. I remember vividly making the announcement at midnight that the party was over and inviting them all to stay for the pre-Christmas mass that we were going to celebrate.

Silence. No one moved. Thinking that they were all going to stay, we started setting up for the mass. Suddenly, as if on cue and without a word being spoken, all the young people except one young man silently headed out the door and into the night. The one who stayed did not receive communion. That strange occurrence remains a mystery to me and to the team. We all had theories but no concrete answers. I do know that I was fascinated by this turn of events. I never forgot it, and perhaps I am still hoping that somewhere along the line, an answer might emerge through my commitment to this kind of ministry.

The second event involved a silent meeting. In the spring of 1972, the Oblates decided to relocate the scholasticate to Edmonton, Alberta, as part of Newman Theological College. The question of what to do with the club arose and was discussed among us as leaders. Given the energy it was taking to keep the club going, some were all for closing it down immediately. Others, including me, wanted to at least hold a meeting with the youth to present the situation to them and see what they wanted to do.

That decision set the stage for the strangest meeting I have ever experienced. We explained the situation to the members and gave them a choice: we could shut the club down now, or they would have to truly take on full responsibility and run the club themselves. We would help them make the transition, but we would not do any of their work for them. Then we stopped talking and waited for their response.

Unlike before the Christmas mass, no one left. But no one spoke, either. Everyone sat in stunned silence for at least ten minutes, allowing this new reality to sink in. I remember one member of the team passing me a note on which she had written, "Scratch the club." I folded it up and waited, sensing that something was happening in the silence. Then, suddenly, Sandra Belanger spoke up and simply said, "OK, I'll do it. What do I have to do?"

Suddenly, the room came to life and everyone burst into conversation simultaneously. I realized with some excitement that what had happened in the silence was a psychological transfer of power from us to the members of the club. For the first time in the history of the club, they knew we were serious in telling them that they really would have to be in charge, and they accepted that responsibility.

We helped them choose an executive, wished them well, and left them to continue to make their plans for a new future without us. We attended the weekly gatherings for the next few months and were surprised by a farewell party they threw for us in May. The club did continue for some time after we left, though I heard later that politics intervened and eventually caused its demise.

The two events described above were instrumental in planting within me a fledgling call to ministry among the First Nations and Métis people.

That first summer at Battleford, the Oblate missionary at Saddle Lake, Alberta, asked me to spend the summer there teaching catechism at nearby Good Fish Lake First Nation. In the process of this work, I became very close to the Anderson family, who lived across the street from the small rectory in Saddle Lake. When I was ordained three years later, I invited them to the celebration in North Battleford and was disappointed when they did not attend. I later learned that they had made it as far as the border town of Lloydminster before turning back, afraid they would not fit in and be accepted at such a "white" event. Their feeling of being "outsiders" gave me a deeply rooted desire to do what I could to change the circumstances that would lead such a beautiful family to feel that way about themselves and towards mainstream society.

The following three summers were spent running youth camps in Île-à-la-Crosse in northern Saskatchewan. I am still amazed that I survived three days in the bush responsible for 42 boys ages twelve to fourteen with only five DNR tents, a cook tent, an outdoor cooking fire and no toilets. A bonus one summer was a free flight into the Dené community of Cree Lake with Fr. James Fiori OMI after the camps were over. Dropped off by firefighters who would pick us up three days later, we enjoyed an idyllic stay in the little log cabin built by a Norwegian trapper that served as a rectory. I even got to use a hand-carved neck yoke that made hauling water up from the lake a breeze.

In 1975, I was assigned to Beauval as a newly ordained Oblate missionary priest. I was now at home in the north and no longer merely a summer visitor. Not only that: I was drawn into the pastoral life of this sprawling missionary archdiocese that covers over 144,000 square kilometres in northern Saskatchewan and Manitoba, as well as a corner of northwest Ontario.

The western side of the archdiocese is a land of sand, evergreen trees, muskeg bogs and sparkling lakes, sliced diagonally into two parts by the Canadian Shield, which begins abruptly around a bend on the Churchill River just east of Pine House Lake. It becomes a land of craggy rocks, muskeg, lakes and trees that unfolds eastward across northern Manitoba to Hudson Bay.

I realized with awe that this was the land the first bishop of this territory, Ovide Charlebois, traversed by foot, train, dog sled, truck and canoe early in the 20th century. Fr. Gaston Carriere OMI, in his book *Le Père du Keewatin*, describes a trip that Bishop Charlebois made in 1911:

> [He] left The Pas in the month of May and returned home four months later. During this trip, he traveled 300 miles by train, 80 in a big truck without springs on terrible roads; 2,000 miles by canoe, 50 miles on foot across portages and thick forest. He slept 60 nights on the ground in a small canvas tent. He visited 14 missions comprised of 4,500 First Nations Catholics. Six of the missions had never been visited by a bishop. He preached seven retreats of 4 to 6 days and confirmed 1,100 First Nations persons whose dispositions were edifying. He noted with sadness

the inadequate number of missionaries. In a dozen communities, the people were asking for a priest.

Though mines and minerals from uranium to nickel abound in this huge land, the most precious resource is its people. Boasting only a few cities, such as Flin Flon and Thompson in Manitoba, the landscape is dotted with First Nations and Métis communities, some connected by sand, gravel or paved roads, others only by air. Each community is distinct and unique, facing many challenges and featuring many creative ways of meeting these challenges.

After about three years in Beauval, changing needs and personnel led to my involvement with the communities of Île-à-la-Crosse, Canoe Lake, Cole Bay and Jans Bay, Saskatchewan, as well as monthly weekend ministry in Pine House. Having a residential school in Beauval attended by students from across the north helped me meet and get to know parents from almost all the communities. The variety of movements in the Church as well as the diocesan gatherings seemed to create a large family that I was able to experience first locally, and then as part of a travelling archdiocesan renewal team.

In 1990, I took a two-year break from ministry for some personal renewal time in the States. When I returned to Canada, I joined a First Nations ministry team in and around the Battlefords in the adjoining diocese of Prince Albert, Saskatchewan, which also had been started by the Oblates. As the communities we served in that diocese were in the heart of the Plains Cree culture, ministry took on a more nomadic and externalized flavour. This was the land of powwows, sun dances, round dances, give-away dances and feasts, and a lot of visiting in the seven communities we served.

After a year-long period of Cree language learning in 1999, as part of the Plains Cree Oblate Community in Saddle Lake, Alberta, I returned to Saskatchewan in 2000 to form the Cree Nation Oblate community with two other Oblates. We served the area of Loon Lake, or *Mâkwa Sâkahigan*, as it is known in Cree. It was here that Mother Church found me and set the process in place that saw me return to the Archdiocese of Keewatin-The Pas in the fall of 2005, this time as their co-adjutor archbishop.

With all that experience and history begging to be expressed, the occasion of my 25th anniversary of priesthood in 1999 gave me the nudge I needed to finally start writing. These stories are a modest attempt to record and share some of the more significant events and characters that peopled the fifteen years (1975–1990) that I spent as a missionary Oblate priest in the Archdiocese of Keewatin-The Pas, the years I spent ministering in the diocese of Prince Albert (1992–1998 and 2000–2005), as well as a few stories from after my episcopal ordination. To be faithful to the chronology of developments, however, I begin with one story from my first summer of First Nations ministry in Saddle Lake. As you will discover, it provided the foundation for my desire to make a commitment to First Nations ministry.

As I look back over those years, I am in awe of how God has worked in the lives of the communities and in my own life.

The Church, for me, was a dynamic and healing reality that drew out the best of its members and truly felt like the beginnings of the reign of God in our lives. I will always be grateful for those years and those times of growth as a people. Much of what happened is due to the tremendous openness and willingness of the people of the north to follow the prompting of the Spirit in new ways. The whole experience reminds me of the words of the founder of my Oblate community, St. Eugene De Mazenod: "Leave nothing undared."

These are stories of inspiration, of realism, of faith meeting life that may help someone else on their journey of faith. I also hope that reading these stories may inspire especially First Nations and Métis youth to consider a life of committed service in the Church as a priest, religious or dedicated lay person.

Read on and enjoy.

+ *Sylvain Lavoie, OMI*

Drumming from Within

The request was simple. The pastor of the First Nations parish in Saddle Lake, Alberta, wanted a hard-working scholastic to teach catechism to the children at the adjacent Good Fish Lake First Nations community.

When asked if I would consider this request, I immediately accepted. I could hardly contain my excitement. This was exactly what I was hoping for as a summer ministry!

As soon as I arrived, I settled into the front room of the rectory. That small room was now not only a sitting room but also my office and bedroom for the next six weeks.

Across the road lived the Anderson family, consisting of four generations: *Kokum* (Cree for "grandmother"), Jeannie and her sister Irene, Jeannie's daughters Velma, Theresa and Patsy and a son, Eugene, as well as Velma's son Little Joe. They were very welcoming and I quickly felt part of their family.

The work of faith education in Good Fish, a half-hour away, began as I visited every home in the community, inviting parents to send their children to the catechism classes that would be held at the church. On weekends I would travel with the pastor, Fr. George Lagrange OMI, to the community for Sunday Eucharist, where I would meet the children and their parents.

The kids were quiet and well behaved, perhaps a little awed at this stranger who had come from another province to work with them as a scholastic brother. Classes were held outdoors whenever possible. I remember planting corn in a basin to illustrate the Parable of the Sower; the corn grew rather well over those six weeks.

What was most striking about my venture into another culture was what happened after my six weeks were over. The Anderson family invited me back to attend the Indian Days, a traditional powwow being held that fall in the community.

I left our summer camp at Lac-des-Îles to return for that event. I spent the weekend, free from all commitments, hanging out with the Anderson children and teenagers. They gave me a blanket and I danced as much as I wanted after taking all the pictures that my heart desired with my Pentax camera. Years later, I continue to delight in watching those slides that are now on the screen saver of my computer.

A powwow is a colourful event that gathers hundreds of people – young and old, elders and grandparents, parents and helpers, drummers, singers and dancers. The exquisite costumes, the intense faces of the dancers and their expressive movements are a gift for anyone who loves to take photographs.

The final night of the powwow saw me up on the bleachers, wrapped snugly in my blanket because of the cool night air. I was tired from all the dancing and content just to sit and watch, drinking in the sights and sounds of the event. I became aware of the fresh autumn smell and feel that was creeping up on us all as a gentle hint that another season, winter, was on its way.

As midnight drew near, the arbour grew crowded with dancers of all ages circulating in the traditional clockwise direction. Feathers, bustles, beaded outfits, colourful shawls, leather moccasins, headdresses and painted faces all competed for my attention. The drums beat on incessantly. The sharp high-pitched jangle of the cones on the jingle dresses mingled with the harsher bells on the leather leggings of the male dancers. The singing seemed to convey a subtle increase in intensity. The faces suddenly became a sea of humanity, moving, pulsating, undulating, mesmerizing, all in time with the beating of the drums.

Suddenly, or perhaps not so suddenly, it was as if I was in a trance, transported into another space and time. There was a feeling of peace, of oneness, of communion, as if we were all one body, one people under the autumn sky. I ceased to hear the drumming with my ears. Instead, it felt as if the drumming was coming from within me, from somewhere deep in my soul, throbbing out a primordial heartbeat.

Something happened, or shifted, within my being that night. I would never be quite the same. I think it was then that my calling to work among the First Nations and Métis people was conceived and born. I really never questioned it later. It somehow just seemed understood, even by my Oblate superiors and confrères, that I would eventually minister among the First Nations and Métis peoples, even though at that time our Oblate province did not have any Aboriginal ministry.

And so it was to be. For over 30 years I have ministered among the First Nations and Métis peoples in both northern Saskatchewan and Manitoba, perhaps all because of that night in Saddle Lake, when the drumming came from within.

Scripture

David and all the house of Israel were dancing before the Lord with all their might, with songs and lyres and harps and tambourines and castanets and cymbals.

(2 Samuel 6:5)

Prayer

Lord, you have given us this universe and life on mother earth as your gift. May we respond by giving you praise and glory through song and dance, with instruments of all kinds.
Give us grateful hearts,
and help us to lead lives of loving service and joyful praise. Amen.

Passage to Peace

The return address read: Casa Generalizia, 00100 Roma-Aurelio. It was here at last – my first obedience!

My hands trembled as I opened the letter that contained my immediate future. As missionary Oblates, our first obedience always came from the Superior General in Rome, in consultation with the Canadian regional councillor. Technically, the Superior General could send us anywhere in the world and to any Oblate province, though invariably, one was assigned to one's own province.

This letter held the unexpected. After entering the novitiate and studying under the auspices of St. Mary's Province for five years, I was being assigned to the Vice-Province of Keewatin-The Pas to work among the Cree First Nations and Métis people of the north.

How that decision happened wasn't a great concern for me. I suspect there was some politicking by the provincial and some partiality by the regional councillor, as I had spent the previous three summers doing ministry in the north. However, I was more interested in getting to work right away after months of waiting for that letter from Rome.

My first action was to phone my new provincial, Fr. Vianney Belanger OMI, who was probably as surprised as I was. On an impulse, I took the initiative and asked if I could first of all learn Cree. Though our studies at the seminary did not include missiology, I had grasped the importance of learning the culture and language from missionaries such as Fr. Richard Doll OMI of South Africa. The provincial agreed to my request and suggested I go to Beauval, where Fr. Rho OMI would teach me Cree.

A friend took most of my belongings to my new home; I hitch-hiked up later with a suitcase and guitar. Especially memorable was the unbroken 100-kilometre stretch of sand and gravel road between Green Lake, where the road turns north, and Beauval. For over an hour, the road unfurled like a ribbon flanked on both sides by a wall of bright birch, colourful poplar and stately evergreen trees, with only one solitary trapper's cabin midway. It was like a passage to another world. In time I would realize not only how true those words were, but also how profound that passage into another culture would be.

Amisk-sîpîsis, the Cree name meaning "Little Beaver River," was a small Métis community on the edge of the beautiful Beaver River valley; hence, the English name taken from the French (Beau-val). The majestic Beauval Indian Residential School, as it was called at that time, stood across the river. Situated on the southern portion of the English River First Nation, the residence had been rebuilt in 1929 after a fire demolished it.

Nearby, the enchanting La Plonge Creek burbled down through sylvan glades from clear, cold, spring-fed Lac La Plonge, silently glided past the residence, where it provided pure drinking water, shot over the unique, picturesque dam built by the Oblate brothers, and finally flowed into its destination, the meandering Beaver River.

After about two weeks in my new home of Beauval, it became obvious that my language learning was suffering. Fr. Rho was busy with fall maintenance of the buildings and had not much time to teach the language on short notice to someone who was short on techniques for learning and not the most patient student. A week later, Fr. Rho moved to Pine House, where there was no priest. I was left in charge of a small Métis village, a small First Nations community across the river, and two schools.

I did make one more attempt to go back to language learning: I phoned the provincial to ask if I could go to Chipweyan Lakes in northern Alberta for that purpose. I had heard the Cree was excellent there, and there was a cabin where I could stay. His response was that I should "forget language learning because it wasn't important." I guess that is symbolic of where we were at as Oblates with regard to culture and language back in 1975, a stance that suddenly left me pastor of my first mission.

Although I believe I went north with the right idea – to do little the first year and focus on learning the language – being suddenly responsible for ministry changed everything drastically, at least for me. Some things, such as faith education in both schools, needed to be taken care of immediately. Other needs flowed from there, as they do in any parish. I didn't respond to this challenge so much as react to it. I got busy trying to meet every need that came along with every idea I had. My natural tendency towards being a doer and a workaholic surged to the fore; absorbing the local language and culture quickly faded to the background.

Perhaps the provincial was right. Maybe language and culture weren't that important. After all, the elements usually associated with being "Indian," such as dancing, drums, pow-wows and feather headdresses were not evident. Things seemed fairly "normal" in Beauval. This was a Métis/Cree community, and I felt fairly comfortable, especially with the French part of the Métis reality there. Even the First Nations communities in the area, both Cree and Dené, did not manifest those outward elements either.

What I didn't realize was that I had entered into an "internalized culture." It was just as much another world as that of Brazil or of the Plains Cree people further south. It was a culture not so much of different physical attributes as of different inner attitudes: ways of being, ways of feeling, ways of seeing oneself, ways of expressing oneself; ways of seeing one's community and the outside world. It was a world of different attitudes towards basic and elemental values, such as time, money, work, humour, recreation, family, relationships, education and spirituality.

Initially, I found this subtle reality difficult to grasp. I was left feeling uncomfortable, vulnerable and tense – rather unpleasant feelings. Unfortunately, I had let the focus on cultural awareness slip away when I gave up on formal language learning. As a result, I was not able to process what was going on within me. I reacted in my usual fashion by energetically going on the offensive. I poured myself into ministry and tried to establish some kind of solid ground for myself. I sought for a sense of control, identity, change and progress.

I became very busy, working long days, ministering to people, celebrating liturgies, developing catechetical programs for both the elementary school and high school. It became difficult to find time to relax, have fun or just visit folks – all this in a village of about 500 people. In fact, I began to resent interruptions, such as visits by my Oblate neighbour, elderly Fr. Eduoard Perreault OMI of Canoe Narrows, who would want to chat and play game after game of cribbage during the workday, of all things!

Finally, the day after Christmas that first year in Beauval, I found myself exhausted after hearing countless confessions leading up to midnight mass. I decided to do a *poustinia*, a 24-hour retreat of prayer and fasting, before going south to visit my family. (*Poustinia* is the Russian word for desert.) Yet there was no peace or serenity to be found: only dryness, aridity and an inexplicable feeling of sadness. Without any further discernment of this unusual experience during my retreat, I set off to visit my family.

Usually, my return north after a stay in the south was a pleasant passage from Green Lake to Beauval. This time, however, I found myself grappling with feelings of sadness, resentment and fear.

Unaccustomed to "feeling feelings" at that time, let alone sharing them, I was ill equipped to process what was actually a mild depression. And so I continued as before for the better part of a year, trying hard to appear happy while repressing the tension and lack of happiness inside of me. For the most part, I succeeded. However, some people sensed my lack of peace and at times would make comments such as "Father is burning the candle at both ends." I generally ignored them.

A crack in my armour appeared during an incident in the fall of 1976. I had attended a charismatic conference in Calgary that left me feeling sad. My travelling companions to the Grey Nuns' centre in Edmonton, meanwhile, were overflowing with joy and excitement. I was confused. I asked myself, "Why is this happening?"

The gospel at the Eucharist the next morning was the story of the rich young man. I had always thought that some-one meeting Jesus would go away elated, but this young man went away sad after hearing Jesus invite him to "Give all to the poor, then come follow me," for he had many possessions. It suddenly hit me! I was the rich young man. I also had "met Jesus" at the conference and gone away sad. I, too, must be clinging to some possession.

That insight gave me a clue to my situation, yet left me puzzled. What was my possession? I had put the income from the land I owned in trust when I became an Oblate. I had taken a vow of chastity and was trying to follow Jesus as best I could.

The mystery remained with me for months, though a couple more clues surfaced. For example, one day at the high school I shared with a Christian Ethics class a John Powell video about the "masks" people wear. In the ensuing discussion, the students identified my mask as the Messiah. This was another clue, but I didn't understand it.

And so it continued for months. I was tired and unhappy, stressed and always tense. Every time I went south, it became more difficult to make the return journey on that now lonely Green Lake to Beauval stretch. At times I would feel like turning around. This priestly vocation was harder than I expected. I felt like quitting. In desperation, I phoned Bishop Adam Exner OMI, who had been my spiritual director in the seminary. In a nutshell, he told me that I had to "fail miserably at something and still be accepted by my people." Cryptic and insightful words, but I still didn't understand.

Then another insight came. Sr. Gabrielle gave me a pamphlet by Stuart Briscoe entitled "This Is Exciting," in which he shared his experience of Christianity. He found being a Christian easy, the first 20 years of life. As a seminarian trying to be perfect, however, he found it hard. When he described Christianity as "neither easy nor hard," my curiosity was aroused. I turned the page and read, "It was impossible."

Suddenly it was as if the scales fell from my eyes and I could see! I was trying to do the impossible, under my own power and on my own terms. I realized that I was doing *my* will in God's name and carrying everything on *my* shoulders. God didn't seem to be doing much, so I had to. And I *had* failed miserably at something. I couldn't love the people I was sent to serve. If they came with a problem, it was work and that was okay. But if they came just to visit, like Fr. Perrault, that was an encroachment on my time. I became quite good at communicating my busyness and displeasure nonverbally; soon these visitors would get the message and leave. At about that time, my sister-in-law told me I was afraid to love and be loved. How right she was.

I dropped everything, went jogging in the bush and prayed a prayer of surrender as I had never prayed before. I told the Lord that these were his people and that this was his Church, not mine. I felt a heavy load lift off my shoulders and I was free. That new-found freedom was apparent in the liturgy the following Sunday, as some who attended noticed.

In short, I had "cracked," as they say in the north about outsiders who come from the south. I was able to let go of my own cultural baggage, ideas and goals and accept the reality that was there without feeling a compulsion to change it. I found myself exploring and entering into the attitudes and values that surrounded me and enjoying that new freedom.

I discovered that time is relative and not a god. One definition of Indian time is taking the time that is needed to do what has to be done. Saving money is not a priority, while sharing it with relatives is. It is still in many ways a culture of the poor who are not accustomed to a totally controlled environment. When it is a perfect day and the blueberries are ripe, it is time to go and pick them, even if one has a schedule that says on paper that one is expected elsewhere.

I was impressed by what I saw as the art of grieving and mourning in a public and complete way. A funeral is not finished until the casket has been buried, using ropes and shovels, the dirt nicely rounded and packed down, flowers placed on the grave and a feast or lunch held in the hall. For Aboriginal people, everything centres on relationships: extended family still exists, grandparents are valued and elders never retire. Friends are friends for life.

The world view is one of the sacred. In the Western world view, everything is rational, scientific, technological and explainable. There is very little mystery left. It is as if we militate against mystery. In the world view of Aboriginal people, everything is mystery, sacred, spiritual, and all is related. We are placed here, the most dependent of all creatures, not to dominate the world but to relate to it and to enter into relationship with all of creation. That world view is waiting to be rediscovered. The Western world is now realizing that over-reliance on science and technology has let us down and led to an ecological and economic crisis.

My attitude towards work, time, leisure, humour, family and relationships all began to change. I began to question the culture that had formed that attitude. I began to judge and critique the values of the culture in which I had grown up. I owe an apology to members of my family and to the Oblates with whom I shared these critical remarks for what, I realize now, was a four-year transitional period of acculturation for me.

The sudden death of my father in the fall of 1980 completed this transition, providing the final insight I needed. He died on September 7, right in the middle of the harvest, and was buried in our home parish of Delmas, Saskatchewan, on September 10, a beautiful, warm fall day. Later that day, after the funeral and reception, my brother Louis announced that he was going harvesting. I couldn't believe what I had heard. We had just buried our father. "How can you do that?" I asked him.

His answer was simple: "That's what Dad would have wanted." So off he went, leaving me in shocked disbelief. However, the next morning I decided to go check on the harvest and ended up joining in and harvesting all day. My feelings were in turmoil. How could I be doing this? My father had just been buried and here I was working as if nothing was unusual. In the north I was accustomed to everything stopping for wakes and funerals. I was torn and confused.

That night it rained. The next day I returned north in the rain. As the grey clouds hung somberly overhead and poured out their contents, it slowly dawned on me that we had done the right thing. Imagine the damage there would have been to the grain and the loss that would have been incurred had we not harvested when we did.

It was then that I understood. I was involved with two different cultures, two different worlds, two different economies. In the north, when someone dies, everything stops and everyone gathers together for the wake and funeral. That is appropriate in the north; the fish, the muskrat, the beaver, the deer and moose will still be there days later and come to no harm. But it is not appropriate for the south, where the precious grain must come in quickly when it is dry to retain its quality and value.

I realized that it wasn't a matter of one culture over the other. It was a question of appreciating both as gift, valuing both and being enriched by both. I began to realize that cross-cultural adaptation is part of the reality and richness of the Aboriginal peoples. They are always involved, day after day, in a cross-cultural experience. They have no choice. The dominant non-Aboriginal society bombards them constantly from every direction the moment they wake up. The list is endless: the media, teachers, church people, service workers, government officials and others. That constant cross-cultural exposure takes energy, but it also enriches, and that is part of their ethos as Aboriginal people in this country that once was theirs only.

I began to see the depth and richness that exists for one who decides to enter into and live in an Aboriginal culture. We usually have a choice. We can choose to enter into the unfamiliar world of the "other," or remain safe and secure in our own familiar little world, society and lifestyle. Unfortunately, most of us stay within our own cultural walls. However, that can change. We can choose to enter into the world view of Aboriginal people, into their lives, their social reality, their culture and spirituality. We can choose to go to a powwow, round dance, feast, wake or funeral of someone we know. We can choose to enter into relationships, to become friends with the people and to experience their values and lived reality. That cross-cultural experience came to me not so much by choice as by chance, but I am grateful for all that it has taught me. I would encourage us all to make the choice of cross-cultural experience.

As I returned home after my father's funeral that day in 1980, I realized that I had come full circle. Both cultures were right, just different. I had come to accept them both, and would now be able to live peacefully in both. This time, that solitary tree-walled passage between Green Lake and Beauval was transformed into a welcoming, inviting transitional journey. Coming home had become a two-way passage to peace. Acculturation had happened. I could now journey and minister in peace.

Scripture

He is the image of the invisible God, the firstborn of all creation; for in him all things in heaven and on earth were created, things visible and invisible ... all things have been created through him and for him. He himself is before all things, and in him all things hold together. He is the head of the body, the church.

(Colossians 1:15-18)

Prayer

*Creator God and loving Father,
you who created all things through Jesus your Son,
grant us a Spirit of love for you, each other, ourselves and all of creation.
Help us walk humbly in relationship with all created things.
Help us respect the cultures and world views that differ from ours. Amen.*

A Community Poised to Heal

Every now and then circumstances reveal the uniqueness of a community.

Shortly after landing in St. Theresa Point, a northern Manitoba Ojibway/Cree community, our Keewatin Renewal Team was invited to appear on the local closed-circuit television station. We were asked to give an impromptu introduction of ourselves: who we were and what we would be doing in the community.

The Parish Renewal sessions that took place over the next five nights were well attended. The sessions consisted of music, singing, storytelling, prayer, scripture, teachings and much sharing in small groups and plenary sessions. The community's desire to continue previous community-building efforts, sparked by the Manitoba Oblate Mobile Team, was evident.

During one of the sessions, a woman named Leanna approached Angie Mihalicz, the female member of our team, to share that she had been sexually abused as a child. Leanna felt the need to share this with the community, yet up to that point had not dared to share it even with her own husband, fearing he might get upset or not listen.

Angie wisely responded that the decision would be up to Leanna, and that we as a team would support her totally should she choose to share this personal information publicly. She did just that when the floor was opened up to the participants. With Angie by her side, one hand on Leanna's shoulder, Leanna courageously disclosed the secret of her abuse that she had carried for so long.

When I heard her pour out her story, I was both glad and afraid. I knew the risk she was taking and wondered how she would feel later. I also wondered how the members of the community would respond. As soon as the session finished, I made my way over to where she was sitting, to check on her.

To my surprise, I could not get near her. She was surrounded by three lines of people, all waiting to give her prolonged, tearful and compassionate hugs. I could feel the healing power of those hugs and almost see new life being poured back into her by the very community that had wounded her.

Two weeks later, we returned to the community for a Christopher Leadership Course, which we had promised to give after the renewal. Leanna was on our minds. How was she doing? we wondered. On arrival, we found that she had tried to sign up for the course but had been turned down by the registration person, who had not attended the earlier sessions. He had not seen her growth and, based on his previous knowledge of her, judged that she was too shy to take the course. Needless to say, we were disappointed and so was she.

That setback did not stop her, however. During the course she made the team an exquisite tablecloth to express her appreciation for her newfound freedom, visited us and extended hospitality. Then, on Saturday evening during one of the lessons, something happened that made us wish even more that she was with us.

Two other ladies, perhaps because of Leanna's example, disclosed that they had been sexually molested by a prominent member of the community who was now deceased. The emotions and tears that followed led us to take two unscheduled breaks to deal with the pain of these disclosures. By midnight, we were only halfway through lesson nine. We decided to interrupt the session, which we had never done before. Would we be able to pick it up again the next day with the same spirit? we asked ourselves.

Our fears were unfounded. The class members returned the next day after the Sunday eucharistic celebration on foot, by car, by truck or by snowmobile and carried on as if we had never been interrupted. We sailed through sessions nine and ten, took a short preparation break, and held the graduation banquet. Leanna was there, helping out at the banquet.

Around ten o'clock, as the banquet was drawing to a close, the group told us that they always had a prayer meeting Sunday night. Tired as we were, we cleared the floor, gathered in a circle and proceeded to sing and pray for an hour.

What a unique and special close to our stay in St. Theresa Point. Through faith and prayer, caring and sharing, this community showed itself ready to continue its movement towards communal healing with only a gentle nudge from the outside. The people there also taught us the importance of creating an environment where it is safe to share. Truly, this was a community poised to heal.

Scripture

They devoted themselves to the apostles' teaching and fellowship,
to the breaking of bread, and the prayers.

(Acts 2:42)

Prayer

Lord, we come to you through one another.
Grant us the raw courage and humble honesty
to share our weakness with others,
so that they may in turn be freed to share their weakness with us
and that together we might heal and grow. Amen.

(Adapted from Jean Vanier)

A Prophetic Gesture

"Someday, Father, I'll be ready to give a message in church."

Actions speak louder than words.

James Smith is an elder in the northern Saskatchewan Métis/Cree community of Pine House. A burly fisherman, and an alcoholic in the past, he was at the time of this story quite involved in the Church. Years earlier, he had undergone a conversion experience, had changed his ways and now enjoyed sharing his sobriety with the community. This he does in a unique way, which I knew.

I should have been forewarned when he informed me that he was preparing a message he wanted to share with the people when he was ready.

One Sunday, that moment came. Just before the liturgy began, he said that he would like to speak after I was finished. I agreed, cut my homily short and invited him to address the gathered community.

41

James came up and stood behind the altar to my left. He began to talk with deep emotion about his life as an alcoholic. As he spoke, he bent down and picked up a brown paper bag that was placed on the floor. He reached into the bag, took out a full bottle of whiskey and set it on the altar. There was a gasp from many in the congregation. I believe an elderly woman left the church, shocked that there would be a bottle of whiskey on the altar.

Unperturbed, James continued to describe how, for years, the bottle had been his god, wreaking great damage on him, his family, his livelihood, and the community. At one point, his emotions seemed to overcome him. Leaning on the altar, he paused for a long, silent moment. Then, suddenly, he walked around the altar and headed for the tabernacle where the reserved sacrament was kept.

I thought he was going to pray there for a moment to gain strength, but it was not so. To my shock, he opened the tabernacle, took out the ciborium containing the consecrated hosts, and walked back with it through the church. He placed the ciborium on the altar right beside the whiskey bottle and resumed his talk. At that point I think a few more people left the church. However, being in a bit of a daze myself, I couldn't be sure.

James then spoke about how he had found Jesus and how that experience had changed his life. Jesus was the centre of his life now and had saved him from his addiction. He told the attentive congregation that he had no need of the bottle anymore. He then picked up the bottle, turned to the nearby open window (from which he had earlier removed the screen), took the cap off the bottle, and purposefully poured the contents out the window.

There was not a sound, not a movement in the church. Everyone could hear the gurgling of the whiskey. All eyes were fixed on him as he calmly emptied the bottle. When it was all gone, he put the bottle away in the paper bag at his feet and continued to speak about his new life as a recovering alcoholic with Jesus. James shared the joy of his faith in God's love for him, described the peace of his sobriety, and urged all those struggling with alcohol addiction to do embrace sobriety as well.

That afternoon, after the celebration, he came over to the rectory to visit. We talked about his dramatic gesture and its meaning. It was then that I began to understand its purpose and the motive behind it.

"Father," he told me, "the young people in this village have never seen hard liquor poured out and disposed of in that way. All they have seen is its consumption and felt its disastrous consequences. They will never forget this action, this sight of liquor being thrown away and Jesus literally taking its place."

As I reflected later on some of the dramatic gestures of the Old Testament prophets, I could not help but think and hope that this, too, was a gesture that would bear fruit in this community, as James claimed it would. I also hoped that here in this community, where so many have struggled with alcohol for so long, these prophetic actions would speak louder than words.

Scripture

By contrast, the fruit of the Spirit is love, joy, peace, patience, kindness, generosity, faithfulness, gentleness and self-control. There is no law against such things. And those who belong to Christ Jesus have crucified the flesh with its passions and desires.

(Galatians 5:22-24)

Prayer

Father, as your servant Moses raised up a bronze serpent
on a standard in the desert,
you have raised up your Son Jesus on the cross.
The bronze serpent without poison in it
was a symbol of your son Jesus who, free from addiction,
is the source of our healing.
As we journey through our own personal deserts,
help us to look upon him with faith and experience his freedom. Amen.

Abraham's Sweater

History feels at home in Île-à-la-Crosse. This community of 1,500 Métis/Cree people sees itself as a crosssroads in time. It is sprawled across a peninsula of barren sand jutting into Île-à-la-Crosse Lake. Its Cree name, *Sâkitawak*, is derived from the fact that the lake welcomes the waters of the Canoe River and the Aubichon arm.

Tracing its origins back to the Fort Black Trading Post of 1776 and the first Catholic mission of 1846, this very political and active village celebrated its bicentennial the same year as the United States: 1976.

Appropriately situated at the heart of the village is an elders' lodge. The lodge not only carries much of the oral history of the area but also houses some rather unforgettable characters. Abraham Ratt, a short, stocky energetic elder who took delight in exploring and using traditional medicines such as rat root and rose hip tea, was one such character.

It was our task as pastors to regularly visit the lodge and celebrate the Eucharist with the residents. On one such occasion, I took my sweater off because it was always too hot for me in the lodge. I placed the sweater on the arm of the chair where Abraham was sitting.

This was no ordinary sweater: it was pure wool, a ram's head creation with a zipper that went all the way up into a roll-down collar. A confrère had given it to me as a Christmas present the previous year.

As I placed the sweater beside him, Abraham said, "Nice sweater, Father." Aware of the cultural value of giving an object to anyone who obviously likes it, I jokingly said to him, "Abraham, if you really like it, it's yours." I then went about visiting the elderly in their rooms as they slowly gathered for the Eucharist. Each celebration was a unique experience, with the elderly reading, singing and praying in French, Cree, English and sometimes a little Dené. Île-à-la-Crosse is one of the few places where I have heard three languages used in one sentence: "Please *kipaha la porte!*" ("Please shut the door!").

After the celebration ended and I was packing things up, I went to the chair to get my sweater. Abraham was sitting with his arm on it so I stood by rather obviously, chatting with a resident and waiting for him to give me my sweater.

When nothing happened, I edged a little closer. Abraham glanced up, put the sweater on his arm and said, "Thank you,

Father." I was shocked. He had taken me seriously and intended to keep it! "Oh no, my sweater!" I thought in a moment of panic.

Off to the side, however, I heard Elizabeth Bouvier, the venerable and dignified matriarch of the lodge and the community, comment in French, "*Tsk, tsk, ce n'est pas correcte, ça. On va faire quelque chose.*" ("That's not right. We will do something.") With relief, I thought to myself, she has noticed and will find a way to get my sweater back. The following week and the week after that, I returned to the lodge for the usual visit and celebration, hoping that my sweater would be waiting for me, but nothing. Not a word was said. I just kept on hoping as Christmas approached.

Then, one Saturday, a week before Christmas, I arrived at the lodge to find two nicely wrapped boxes. My name was on one and my brother Oblate's name was on the other. The elderly folk all gathered around, eager for me to open mine. In the box was not my sweater, but a beautiful Siwash sweater with native designs and my initials, S.L., stitched into the design on the back in large letters. Elizabeth had taken up a collection with the residents and all the visitors to the lodge. She commissioned one of the elderly ladies in the village, Victoria Daigneault, to make sweaters for both my confrère and me, as a replacement for the one I had lost. Along with the sweater came a card with the names of all those who had contributed. There at the end of the list was Abraham's name, along with a note giving his donation: $2.

With mixed emotions, still missing my special sweater yet grateful now for this replacement, I told this story to the parish council in Beauval, my other mission. After Christmas Eve mass there the following week, Abraham Gardiner, chairman of the council, presented me with a package. When I opened it, I found a sweater identical to my first one. Apparently, after hearing the story of how I lost my sweater to elder Abraham, the members of the parish council in Beauval searched for one in Meadow Lake and bought it as their Christmas present to me.

The cultural lesson in this incident leads me to adapt a well-known lesson from the Scriptures: "Give, and it will be given to you ...; for the measure you give will be the measure you get back" (Luke 6:38).

Scripture

God loves a cheerful giver. And God is able to provide you with every blessing in abundance, so that by always having enough for everything, you may share abundantly in every good work.

(2 Corinthians 9:7-8)

Prayer

Generous Lord, you have gifted us with all of creation,
life itself and each other.
Grant us an abiding sense of gratitude and a generous spirit
in sharing with others the blessings you have given to us. Amen.

Louis, Moses and Jesus

Have you ever been told to "forget the past" or "let sleeping dogs lie"?

Experience has taught me that dealing with the past is much more positive and life giving than these phrases suggest.

The year was 1977. There had been an AA Round-Up in the village of Beauval, and Louis O. had stayed overnight with friends. Tall and handsome in his leather beaded jacket, Louis stepped into my office the next day for a visit.

He shared some of his story. An alcoholic for twelve years, he had found Alcoholics Anonymous and sobered up. For the next four years, taken up with this new program, he travelled the north, trying to spread the message of AA. In fact, that was how I met him. He had chaired the first AA meeting ever held in Île-à-la-Crosse, where I had gone as a scholastic in the summer of 1972 to run a summer boys' camp.

Then, suddenly, he ended up in the hospital with a heart condition. That experience gave him an opportunity to reflect on his life and his newfound sobriety. It dawned on him that though he was sober now, not much else had changed in his life. He was still tense, worried, empty – often miserable, if the truth were told – and his family was no better off. At times they wished that he were drinking again. He realized that he had been on a "dry drunk" for four years, and was not really working the program.

That realization brought a new resolve to really work the 12 Steps. With a deeper understanding of his own powerlessness, his faith in God's power to heal him grew stronger (Steps 1-2). He made a decision to surrender his life and will to that Higher Power (Step 3). Then Louis signed himself out of the hospital, threw away his heart medication and continued this new way of life with a searching and fearless moral inventory of his whole life (Step 4). Next he shared that painful truth with God and another human being (Step 5).

He then went on to deal with his anger and resentment by learning to forgive those who hurt him, as well as with the losses in his life through acceptance (Steps 6 and 7). He made amends as best he could to the people he had hurt (Steps 8 and 9) and finally began to experience peace and freedom (Steps 10 to 12). As he ended his story, he asked if we could pray together, which we did. Then he left.

After the door closed behind him, I sat there for some time in silent wonder, amazed at the transformation in this man. I marvelled at how it had happened through the 12-Step

Program. But there was more to it than that. Another faint, tantalizing thought was teasing my mind and continued to haunt me for days until it dawned on me. Louis' story was familiar because I had heard it before.

The Exodus account! Louis had experienced the same transforming reality in his life as the Hebrew people in the desert. Their story was one of centuries of slavery and then political liberation as they crossed the Red Sea. Next came Mount Sinai and the Ten Commandments, followed by 40 years of wandering in the desert, where they learned two important things: to trust God one day at a time (manna in the morning; quail every evening) and to look upon a bronze serpent raised on a standard when they were bitten (the bronze serpent had no poison in it). That serpent on a standard is a symbol of the Higher Power in whom there is no addiction. (Those who profess the Christian faith would naturally see this standard as a prophetic prefiguring of Jesus, the sinless one, hanging on the cross.) Finally, after learning these key lessons and teachings, the Hebrew people crossed over the Jordan River and entered the Promised Land.

The similarity between the two stories was striking. For the Israelites, there were six stages of *deliverance*: slavery in Egypt, liberation through the Red Sea, Mount Sinai and the Ten Commandments, a 40-year desert experience, crossing the Jordan, and entering the Promised Land.

For Louis, there were six stages of *recovery*: addiction, sobriety, the 12-Step Program, four years as a dry drunk, recovery, and finally happy, free sobriety. He had been through an Exodus experience.

As I reflected on this new awareness, I felt an intuition that there was more. Then suddenly I realized what it was – the Paschal mystery. That familiar story reveals the same pattern as the previous two stories. Louis had experienced the Paschal mystery, a life-transforming event that was foreshadowed by the Exodus.

For Jesus, the Paschal Lamb, there were six stages of *transformation*: passion (his suffering on the Cross), death, resurrection, appearances to his disciples, ascension into heaven, and Pentecost (the sending of the Spirit on his followers). It was the same pattern, only much deeper, more personal and laden with potential for us. Louis had experienced the Paschal mystery through the 12 Steps.

His years of active addiction were his passion. Sobriety was his death to alcohol. Finding the 12-Step Program was his resurrection, enabling him to survive. Working the Steps, dealing with his hurt and grieving his loss were the appearances of Jesus for him. Forgiving the hurt, letting go of the anger and accepting the losses in his life were his ascension. Experiencing a new life of happy free sobriety and genuine recovery was now his Pentecost.

Over the years I have learned that it is the same for all of us, addicted or not. We can enter into the same six stages of healing life's hurts and transforming our lives into greater peace, joy and freedom by living our faith and working the 12 Steps.

Our passion is our life's *hurts*, leaving us angry and resentful. Our death is the *losses* in our lives, leaving us sad, full of self-pity and often stuck in grief. Our resurrection is our coping skills that enabled us to survive. The problem is that surviving life is not enough. Too many people settle for survival, which is similar to remaining a victim. We are meant to live life to the full, not merely survive it. The Big Book of Alcoholics Anonymous puts it this way: "We have survived life; now we must learn to live it." St. Irenaeus expressed much the same thing in different words: "The glory of God is man and woman fully alive."

The *appearances* become for us a time of healing and grieving, and help us move beyond survival. Jesus appeared to Mary Magdalene and his disciples to teach them to grieve and mourn his loss. He was the same Jesus, but he had changed. Now he was the Risen Lord. However, he could not send them his Spirit unless they let him ascend to the Father. That was why he told Mary Magdalene not to cling to him. She was to have faith that, although she would no longer be able to see him, he would be more present to her through his Spirit than he had been before.

That same lesson is what Jesus wants to teach us. We also must deal with our hurt by expressing our anger in a positive, loving manner, and face our losses by grieving and mourning them. We are finally able to forgive the hurt by letting go of the anger, and to accept the losses by letting go of the sadness and self-pity. In so doing, we create a space into which God can pour the spirit of forgiveness, the spirit we need for whatever loss we have experienced. Through this *forgiveness and acceptance,* our ascension happens.

In the case of loss of a loved one, we receive their spirit to be with us in a new way when we have truly let them go and have given them back to God. We are then ready to experience Pentecost as a *new life* of peace, joy and freedom. We will have had an experience of our own Paschal mystery, an experience of deep inner healing, as did Louis.

So, forgetting the past and letting sleeping dogs lie is not the real answer. Dealing with our hurt and loss through an active faith is. The 12-Step Program, available to all, is a ready guide for anyone wanting to really live life to the full, rather than just survive it. Happy healing journey!

Scripture

Why do you look for the living among the dead? He is not here, but has risen. Remember how he told you, while he was still in Galilee, that the Son of Man must be handed over to sinners, and be crucified, and on the third day rise again.

(Luke 24:6-7)

Prayer

Lord, you are the Messiah who suffered for us.
Give us the faith to find you in our own stories,
our own suffering and loss.
Help us to believe that whatever happened to us happened to you
and that you can walk with us on our own healing journey,
touching our wounds with forgiveness and healing,
so that we can rise to a new life of freedom, peace and joy. Amen.

Note: Louis O. has since passed away. Not surprisingly, at his funeral the church was packed with people who had been touched by his life, faith, courage, humility, generosity and love. How I wish I could have been there to add my own testimony to his goodness and celebrate his life. Though that was impossible, may the relating of this story be my part in spreading the legacy of this beautiful human being who lived an exemplary life of recovery, unity and service.

Mr. Duffy's Conversion

"It is better to light one candle than curse the darkness."

Let your light shine in the small, ordinary events of every-day life.

Suzy Berthelette was a young girl living in a northern Manitoba village. Each day she would bounce down the stairs, go the fence in the backyard and call out a greeting to the next-door neighbour, a mean old man named Mr. Duffy, who hated kids.

In spite of Mr. Duffy's crabbiness, Suzy would go to the fence every morning, look over and call out, "Hi, Mr. Duffy, how are you?" And every day he would reply with some sort of offensive comment, calling her down and putting her off. One day he even sent a note to her mother, warning her that if Suzy didn't stop bothering him, he would shoot at her.

Her brothers and her mother tried to dissuade her, telling her not to go to the fence and bother him. They insisted that he was a mean old man and she should just leave him alone, but to no avail. Every morning she would bounce down the stairs, scoot out the door to the fence and call out her cheery greeting, "Hi, Mr. Duffy, how are you?"

One day when she went to the fence and called out her customary greeting there was no reply. Instead, she heard a low moaning and groaning. Unable to see what was happening, she went to get her mother. Together they ventured into Mr. Duffy's yard to check out the sounds Suzy had heard.

They found Mr. Duffy in his backyard. A tractor tire he had been working on had slipped, pinning him against a tree and slowly crushing the life out of him. Suzy ran home for help while her mother went into Mr. Duffy's house and called an ambulance.

Suzy's brothers quickly lifted the tire off Mr. Duffy and an ambulance whisked him to the hospital, where he recovered from this near fatal accident. The doctor who treated him said that he would most certainly have died had he not been found and helped so fast.

Suzy was a small-town hero. Her persistent friendliness had saved Mr. Duffy's life. This young girl truly let her light shine for all to see. As for Mr. Duffy, he was a changed man. Now, whenever Suzy greeted him, he responded in a friendly manner and sometimes would invite her over for juice and cookies. He never tired of thanking her for her unwavering ability to reach out to others without being discouraged by a negative response. Because of this quality, she had saved his life, in more ways than one.

So remember, it is better to light one small candle than to curse the darkness. Let your light shine in the ordinary events of everyday life.

Scripture

"No one has greater love than this, to lay down one's life for one's friends."

(John 15:13)

Prayer

Lord, give us a love for others
that understands and accepts them as they are
and mirrors your love for us.
Plant and nourish within us your unconditional love,
which overcomes all obstacles to friendship
and seeks nothing in return. Amen.

Kîwetin – Winds of Change

Kîwetin is a Cree word meaning "wind from the north." From this word comes the name of the northern Manitoba-Saskatchewan Archdiocese of Keewatin-The Pas.

The recent history of the community of Île-à-la-Crosse calls that word to mind, for "winds of change" blew through this village in the mid-1970s. Those winds of change had a strong impact on the village itself as well as on ordinary couples and families, such as Jim and Marie Favel.

My first contact with Île-à-la-Crosse was during the summer of 1972, when I went there as a young scholastic for a three-week stint of summer ministry. The tension and ferment of change was in the air. The following year, half of the school burned down. Though the cause is unknown to this day, arson was suspected. The other half of the building was saved by Bro. Bertrand Guay OMI, who drove a steel-treaded Caterpillar tractor through the connecting corridor to cut the building in two and stop the fire from spreading.

That fire and the need to build a new school were catalysts for something big. All kinds of forces suddenly emerged. For one, Aboriginal architect Douglas Cardinal, who had produced a white paper (official report) on Indian education for Indian people, was invited to design a new school. He travelled north to see the location and vigorously promoted his philosophy of Aboriginal education for Aboriginal students.

Another factor was that the newly elected New Democratic Party (NDP) government of Saskatchewan had just created the Department of Northern Saskatchewan (DNS), which sought to give greater autonomy to that vast stretch of land so often neglected by the south. As part of that political climate, many left-wing NDP members had just broken away and formed a more radical Waffle Party. When the NDP formed the government, many of the latter group were sent north, to La Ronge in particular, and so were involved in this new department. They were keen to try new things to bring about social change, and saw the political climate in Île-à-la-Crosse as an opportunity for a social experiment.

As well, the newly formed local and provincial Métis Societies were eager to participate in a share of that greater autonomy. They felt the need to define themselves, their role and their identity in the shaping of northern politics. Local people and leaders spoke sincerely and passionately of the need for the formation of a local school board that would give more say to local people in the education of their children.

To better understand the unfolding of events at that time, however, it must be stated that political influence from the outside had its own agenda, was not above manipulation, and encouraged militancy on the part of the local Métis Societies to achieve their own political ends. Unfortunately, this political reality created an atmosphere of conflict and hostility that led to division, rather than one of dialogue that could lead towards collaboration.

As these new forces and winds of change grew stronger and more pronounced, old attitudes, which had grown imperceptibly over the previous century, stood out in sharp contrast. These attitudes had settled like dust over the settlement and its lifestyle, and had hardened and crystallized over the years.

This situation reminded me of a certain theory of revolution mentioned during Church history class in the seminary at Battleford at about that time. According to the book *The Anatomy of a Revolution*, an ambitious middle class with a new ideology stirs up the lower class to remove the ruling upper class and bring about a change that will gain power for the middle class.

As I observed what was happening during those intense years of flux in Île-à-la-Crosse, I began to relate that theory to the events that we were experiencing. I believe that, with all good intentions and innocently enough, a kind of upper class had developed over the years since 1776. This elite group consisted of mostly Euro-Canadian influential leaders: doctors, nurses, police, Hudson Bay manager, resource management personnel, priests, religious sisters and brothers and, to a lesser degree, because of their short-term residency, teachers. They had the better jobs, sat on most of the boards, held most of the power, and made the key decisions. The local people became, in effect, the lower class according to this theory.

This elite group was also set apart by an invisible wall of socializing and inter-relating that excluded the local Métis people, with few exceptions. Euro-Canadian individuals or couples who did relate and socialize with the local people were shunned by the elite group for doing so. One couple from England who did mix quite a bit almost had to leave because of that subtle yet perceptible social pressure. Another couple, from south-central Saskatchewan, shared with me that they also had experienced that pressure because they mingled with the local people.

On the part of the Church, unfortunately, it must be admitted that the attitude had become paternalistic and colonial mixed in with a strain of cultural superiority. Added to that was a good deal of power, influence and control over the older people and the Church faithful.

Resistance by leaders and members of the Church to these winds of change and shift in power and control was interpreted by some of the more militant political activists as a need to get rid of the Church. That mood was interpreted by those on the Church's side as justification for resisting these forces of change. Symbolic of that attitude was the comment by a Church leader to a CBC reporter that the "Native people were not ready to take over control of their own education." That comment drew the following response from one of the local Métis leaders: "If, after 150 years of mission rule, we are not ready to take control of our own education, when will we be ready?"

While the issue was really about local people having a greater say in their own affairs, these judgments and counter-judgments clouded the issue and further divided the community. Unfortunately, many well-meaning people, who simply wanted a stronger voice in local issues that affected them and who were not against the Church at all, got caught in a confusing crossfire.

What followed were years of tension: some of which was healthy, and some destructive. The community was divided down the middle. Strategy meetings were held on both sides, and a local school board was formed. The newly hired principal and teaching staff became a hotbed of foment and catalysts of change. Social workers became the new outside advisers. Were the teachers and social workers the new middle class of the theory mentioned above?

The one teaching sister who remained on the school staff was made to feel unwelcome. Heated arguments and discussion happened all over the village, and a life was lost in a violent scuffle at a party. Certainly the education of the children suffered. The archbishop, who was called in for a meeting, threatened to pull out all the priests, brothers and sisters. Finally, a short-lived separate school was formed in the basement of the hospital. This last development more or less ended the uprising and began a return to some degree of normalcy in the community.

It was during this intense time that I first met Jim and Marie Favel, an influential couple in the village. While Jim and his brother Jonas were very political, Marie's involvement was with the Church. These events pulled Jim into a political maelstrom that placed pressure on their family, their faith and their marital relationship. The political forces at play actually pitted Jim against the Church to which both he and Marie belonged. While Marie continued to attend church, Jim would be heavily involved in meetings and travels that sought to change the role that the Church was playing in the north.

As time went on, things continued to cool down. The new school board learned from some of its mistakes and proved to be functional. The AA and Al-Anon movements came to the north at that time, and both Jim and Marie became members. Proponents of First Nations spirituality were beginning to move north as well. One such person was Fr. John Hascal OFM from Michigan, a noted charismatic healer and medicine person of Ojibway descent. He celebrated a Eucharist that integrated First Nations spirituality with Catholic Christian faith, attended a sweat lodge at Jim and Marie's, and encouraged them to develop their own Métis sweat lodge.

At the same time, the theology of Vatican II was percolating within the Church and beginning to have an impact on its leaders. Dialogue, inculturation, respect for First Nations spirituality, affirmation of culture and greater local autonomy were key elements of that renewed theology. These new concepts were timely and much needed at this critical historical moment in Île-à-la-Crosse.

Ironically, the younger priests assigned to Île-à-la-Crosse at that time were very much in favour of local control and were working hard to involve people in the development of their own Church. For example, Île-à-la-Crosse in 1970 had one of the first local parish pastoral councils in the whole province, though perhaps this development was too little, too late.

Admittedly, it is difficult for those in a dominant society to truly enter into, feel and understand the issues and lived reality of the minority. As such, these pastoral workers were caught in and unprepared to cope with the unfolding of a political and social phenomenon that was way beyond the scope of regular pastoral activity.

Miraculously, Jim and Marie were able to ride out the storm that threatened to engulf both their community and their family. AA and Al-Anon proved to be life rafts for them. Marie's faith remained strong and served as an anchor for both her and her husband. Support came from the community as true friends stayed faithful. Marie's steady involvement with the Church led to her becoming director of the Northwest Keewatin Pastoral Center in Île-à-la-Crosse for some years, as well as an unofficial counsellor and mentor for many people over and above her regular work.

By 1978, an Advent retreat was held in the school – the first time since 1973 that such an event was possible. New personnel in the school and the Church brought fresh ideas and relationships, which helped heal the wounds from the recent past.

This analysis is and can only be a surface skimming of this phenomenon that took place in a key historical northern community. I chose to include this somewhat still painful subject in this book for two reasons.

One reason is to point out the need for a qualified historian to write as objectively as possible an account of the history of those momentous events that shook this community so deeply for so many years.

The second reason is to draw attention to the fundamental, if painful, lessons so that we as a Church can learn from what happened. Over and over, perhaps, we need to learn to be self-critical and watch for those subtle attitudes of paternalism and colonialism, power and control, domination and cultural superiority that can so easily creep into our lifestyle and ministry. These subtle (and sometimes not so subtle) negative attitudes lead us away from the ideal and spirit of the Beatitudes, which Jesus modelled for us. He always took the side of the poor and chose the way of the cross.

The words of one Oblate involved at that time reflect this humble attitude: "I think we were all doing our best. Sometimes it is through these messy conflicts that we learn from our mistakes and grow the most."

So yes, *Kîwetin*: there is a wind out of the north, a wind that can blow key lessons for life and ministry towards us. It is up to us to draw out those lessons and integrate them into our lives for today.

Scripture

If then there is any encouragement in Christ, any consolation from love, any sharing in the Spirit, any compassion and sympathy, make my joy complete: be of the same mind, having the same love, being in full accord and of one mind. Do nothing from selfish ambition or conceit, but in humility regard others as better than yourselves. Let each of you look not to your own interests, but to the interests of others. Let the same mind be in you that was in Christ Jesus.

(Philippians 2:1-5)

Prayer

*Lord, in the midst of political turmoil
that wanted to see you acclaimed king and ruler,
you remained faithful to the will of the Father.
You showed us a new way:
the way of long-suffering, humble faith
that led you to accept the cross.
Liberate us from the false gods of power, domination and control
in our life and ministry.
Grant us that same spirit of humble faith and loving service of others
that finds you in the least of our brothers and sisters
and in the humblest of their needs. Amen.*

Recovery Lake

"Has anybody seen Leonard?"

"Do you know if there is a Christopher Course today?"

Those were the questions we were asking ourselves as our Keewatin Renewal Team van rolled into Pine House for what was supposed to be the beginning of a leadership course organized by Leonard McCallum.

The answer we received not only made up for our disappointment over not finding him at Pine House, but also piqued our curiosity and interest. It seems that Leonard had suddenly been inspired to take sixteen alcoholics from the community into the bush to sober them up.

Leonard is an exceptional person. The survivor of an alcoholic family, he ended up in the hospital with alcohol poisoning at least three times starting at age fourteen and went through several rehabilitation centres. Creative, gifted as a speaker, facilitator and dancer, and father of a large family, he finally sobered up with the help of Alcoholic Anonymous. Sincerely wanting to change, he participated in any human development sessions he could find. He also took part in faith events that were happening in the Church at that time, such as a Search weekend retreat for youth, the Christopher Leadership Course and a Parish Renewal.

Pine House, the community Leonard grew up in, is a Cree-speaking Métis community southwest of La Ronge on the shores of Pine House Lake, Saskatchewan. Fishing, mining, logging, trapping, rice growing and seasonal firefighting are all part of the people's livelihood. The community has a long history of struggling with alcoholism and home brew. Early efforts to establish Alcoholics Anonymous there by members from neighbouring communities reach back to the mid-1970s, when travel was by air or winter road only.

Leonard's initiative was remarkable and courageous. He invited, cajoled and talked sixteen of the "worst-case scenario" alcoholics of the village into going out to live in the bush for a month. They left with barely enough supplies to get by for a few days: a little food, some tents, tarpaulins, foam mattresses, sleeping bags, blankets, ropes, snare wire, hunting equipment and kitchen utensils. The location Leonard chose was a peaceful glade in the jack pine forest about 15 kilometres south of Pine House, near a small, shallow lake.

Each day, Leonard would catch a ride back into the community to obtain food, supplies and donations from local stores, businesses and community members. Interest in and support for what was happening grew quickly.

Back at the camp, Leonard used every idea he could think of and the experience of his own healing journey to put together a program as they went along. Praying together their own way, sharing their struggles and lives, cooking for themselves and helping each other get by in the bush proved to be a successful formula. They lived on a diet of moose, deer, rabbit, fish, bush partridge and whatever supplies Leonard could get in town.

On his trips back to the village, Leonard invited every resource person he could find to come out to the camp and share what they could about healing, addiction and personal growth. On one such occasion, I was asked to bless the shallow lake. This I did from a boat a little ways off shore. I believe it was at that time that the name "Recovery Lake" was adopted for this unique detox camp.

What a joy it was to visit the camp to see the simplicity of lifestyle as well as experience the honest sharing of painful struggles with life and the devastating effects of alcohol abuse. The renewal of the human spirit was tangible in the setting of nature. Green trees, water, fire, soft, moist fragrant sandy earth, a gentle breeze and bright sunshine all contributed a positive energy. The constant chirping of birds and all the sounds and smells of nature added to that healing force.

Overcoming all obstacles and defying the odds, the group successfully completed the month. The wrap-up was an AA Roundup back in Pine House. A banquet was held, speakers were called up, and each participant received a marble as a symbol of their achievement and as a commitment to ongoing sobriety.

A guest of honour was Sylvia Fedoruk, who was then the lieutenant governor of Saskatchewan. In Pine House for the opening of the summer games, she heard about the Recovery Lake experience, excused herself from a supper with the mayor and council, and came to the Roundup to see for herself. She was amazed and fascinated by this unique and daring venture that survived and succeeded on a shoestring, with no outside financing or government intervention, something almost unheard of at the time.

Two more sessions were held that summer, with one of the original participants serving as a volunteer counsellor. Though less frequent, sessions also took place over the following years. Some months after the first attempt, the Keewatin Renewal Team made it back to Pine House for the Christopher Leadership Course, with some of the original Recovery Lake participants joining the class.

Sadly, not all those who took part in the Recovery Lake movement were able to maintain sobriety. Some have already departed this world. Many, however, look back to that special time in God's creation as a turning point of recovery in their lives. For Pine House and many others, Recovery Lake stands out as a striking example of the power of the human spirit to overcome the odds by discovering inner and external resources, collaborating with others and healing together.

Scripture

He has rescued us from the power of darkness and transferred us into the kingdom of his beloved Son, in whom we have redemption, the forgiveness of sins.

(Colossians 1:13-14)

Prayer

*Lord, give us the faith and courage to make that inner journey
into the heart of our own darkness,
to encounter our inner truth, weakness and sinfulness
as well as our beauty and potential.
Grant us the ability to surrender our lives to you
so that we might find new life and personal freedom
through faith, fellowship and self awareness. Amen.*

Silence and I

She was brought to my attention during First Communion preparation that year. In the end, she taught me a lot about the need for patience and the importance of expressing affection within families.

Sr. Simard SGM, the pastoral worker in Beauval at that time, took me aside one day to inform me that one of the First Communion candidates was a young girl who wouldn't talk. A special approach would be needed for First Reconciliation, which the children celebrated around the same time.

I was incredulous. A Grade 2 child who wouldn't talk? I checked with Len Dupuis, the very understanding school principal, and with the little girl's teacher. Both assured me that it was true: whether in school or out on the playground, Rebecca remained silent. Whenever adults addressed her, her friends came to her defense with the simple statement "She can't talk."

Her family, not given to a lot of communication, told me that at home she did respond a little, but only when spoken to. No one seemed to know why she wouldn't talk at all when outside the home. To her benefit, the community of Beauval accommodated, as it does so well, and over the years learned to live with the girl who wouldn't talk.

When it came time for Grade 9, Rebecca went "across" to the La Plonge Indian Residential High School as a day student, as there was no high school in the village. There she found herself in Angie Mihalicz's English class. Both Angie and her husband, Ed, the principal, had an abundance of patience that turned out to be a blessing for Rebecca.

Angie's approach to teaching English was to get to know her students, so she asked them to write their autobiography as their first assignment. The girl who wouldn't talk could write, and write she did, pouring out her story. Inspired by the Christopher Leadership Course, which teaches a method of praise, evaluation and praise, Angie graded each assignment by praising a skill of the student, contributing value to their effort by suggesting ways of improving, and then adding some personal praise of the student's personality.

That approach worked wonders for Rebecca. She began to hang around Angie's class after school, sometimes doing odd jobs for her, obviously wanting to talk but still not able. With infinite patience, Angie recognized the girl's potential and slowly encouraged her to talk about her autobiography. Little by little, a few words, then short blurts of sentences, started to come out. The girl who wouldn't talk had finally begun to talk!

A few years later, Rebecca participated in a Search weekend at the school residence. An important part of the weekend is an opportunity for the parents and family to express their feelings through a letter about their relationship with their son or daughter, brother or sister Searcher. As chaplain on the team I visited Rebecca's family to stress the importance of that letter and to assist them with it.

One of the sentiments expressed in her family's letter to Rebecca was something like this: "We know that we don't show it very much, but we do love you and care about you." There was a marked change in Rebecca's behaviour that Saturday night after she read those words from her family. She seemed to revert to her old self, retreating into silence behind an invisible wall of aloofness and aloneness. The team was concerned, but the next morning she was all smiles and beaming. It seems that this was the first time she had heard those words expressed to her in that way, and initially she was in shock.

Rebecca continued to grow, to talk more, and to relate to others. To our amazement, she offered to give a talk at one of the Search weekends a few years later. The topic she chose was "Opening Up."

I will never forget that night and the painful way her talk unfolded. After a long silence, Rebecca began by saying, "I couldn't talk for nine years in school," which was followed by another interminable silence. What amazed me most was the way everyone in the room was comfortable with the silence. Each one was very present, waiting, patient, silently supporting her and encouraging her to go on.

And she did go on, quietly inserting a few more short sentences into the long, respectful, expectant silence of that memorable presentation. And then to top it all off, she finished her talk by playing a song popular at that time: "Silence and I." That did it. I don't think there was a dry eye in the place as the girl who wouldn't talk gave her first talk in public to her peers.

Rebecca went on to graduate, get a job, fall in love and marry, and is now raising a family in Alberta. She and her teacher, Angie, remain in my memory as inspiring examples of the power of patience. I also remember how important it is for families to express their love and affection to each other. The girl who wouldn't talk has been transformed for me into someone who speaks that message powerfully: a message we all need to hear again and again.

Scripture

Love is patient; love is kind; love is not envious or boastful or arrogant or rude. It does not insist on its own way; it is not irritable or resentful; it does not rejoice in wrongdoing, but rejoices in the truth. It bears all things, believes all things, hopes all things, endures all things.

(1 Corinthians 13:4-9)

Prayer

Lord, we pray that your patient love and acceptance
working in our lives
may make us more and more sensitive
to the often unspoken needs of the people around us.
Grant us the patience and kindness we need
to be a source of healing for all those
who are unable to articulate their own woundedness. Amen.

Simon Says

Emotions stirred within me as our plane approached the community of Lac Brochet in northern Manitoba. Years earlier, a friend and former Oblate confrère, Claude Sheehy, had moved here from the village of Brochet with the Dené people. They wanted to begin a new life for themselves in this community that had been carved out of the wilderness on the shores of Lac Brochet, not far from the Northwest Territories.

In a valiant and courageous missionary attempt to live with the people and learn the language and culture, Claude had lived in a small log shack that the people had built for him. Now we were here and would be able to see and experience this place and these people he had told us so much about.

After a warm, welcoming meal provided by the pastoral worker, Sr. Lea Desharnais NDN, a problem arose. Small-group sharing was an integral part of the Parish Renewal session we were here to present, but such sharing is difficult in a church full of pews. Sr. Lea had asked to use the community hall for the Renewal session; we would finish up in the church. Yet when we went to set up in the hall, it was obvious that a miracle would be needed. A door was loose; windows were boarded up; one wood furnace was missing and the other one was broken. Two teenage girls were half-heartedly sweeping the dusty floor. When asked about the situation, they informed us that Simon said we should use the church.

Being guests and strangers, our team did not want to impose, so we offered to change our plans and use the church. Sr. Lea, insisting that arrangements had been made for the hall, left to work on that detail while we waited back at the house. Every attempt she made to spur on the clean-up effort, however, was met by the same response: "Simon says we should use the church." So in the end, we set up in the church, wondering all the while who Simon was.

That arrangement worked out well. The people were accustomed to using the church for meetings. When such events took place, they simply pulled a curtain hung on a wire across the front of the church to close off the altar area and form a hall full of movable benches.

We were more than impressed by the faith of the people: elders, adults and youth. Each night began with people of all ages taking turns stepping up to a microphone and leading the rosary crisply and clearly in Dené. We then celebrated the Eucharist and moved right into the sessions.

That Renewal was a memorable experience because of the way the large-group sharing unfolded. As most of the sharing was in Dené, which we did not understand, a man named Simon Samuel came forward to facilitate the speakers. He did so with ease and finesse. We began to understand why people were saying, "Simon says...."

Sensing our need to keep abreast of what was being shared, the chief began to write down on a yellow legal pad what was being said as we looked over his shoulder. And so it went each night for all the sessions. After our initial input, all we had to do was wrap it up at the end.

The last night always closed with a liturgy that featured a dramatized gospel and the renewal of baptismal commitment. Even though we did not have to move from a hall to the church as usual, the celebration lasted until about 10 p.m. As I was unvesting afterwards, I felt a tap on my shoulder. There was Simon, excitedly inviting us to come over to the hall right away. Knowing the state of the hall, which we had seen on Sunday, I hesitated. But seeing his eagerness, I decided to accept.

What a surprise greeted us! The hall had been transformed. A new door and a new furnace were prominent. Tablecloths covered the tables, which were arranged banquet style. Streamers hung from the ceiling. We sat down to a festive, late-night lunch. Apparently, Fred Denecheze and Marie Vallioux had gone door to door throughout the community on an ATV, collecting whatever people could spare for the lunch. We were deeply touched, knowing that these people were struggling to survive in this imposing land and could ill afford extras, especially at the time of the month that we were there.

After the lunch, a variety of people spoke and shared their experience of the sessions. Then Fred led onto the stage a group of singers who entertained us with their favourite hymns in Dené. The generous hospitality, sincere singing, warm fellowship and deep expression of faith gave us an idea that night of what it must have been like for the early Christians as they gathered to celebrate their faith.

Months later, we were moved to learn from their pastor, Fr. Darveau OMI, a veteran missionary who was fluent in both Cree and Dené, that the people had developed their own follow-up to the renewal sessions. Every Saturday night, they gathered as usual for the rosary and Eucharist. Immediately after, they would proclaim the gospel for that Sunday, divide up into small sharing groups and then gather as a plenary to share their faith and their lives with their brothers and sisters in Christ.

Fred and Marie even flew to Wollaston, a neighboring Dené community in Saskatchewan, to share their experience of the Parish Renewal. To top it all off, it was at about this time that members of the Lac Brochet community began to journey from northern Manitoba by plane and across Saskatchewan by chartered bus to attend the July Lac Ste. Anne pilgrimage in Alberta.

What a pleasure it was to see Simon and Fred at Lac Ste. Anne years later, to remember the renewal in Lac Brochet, to share anew their faith journey and to see them celebrating their faith in fellowship with the thousands of other Aboriginal cousins from the four directions.

With a smile, Simon had the last word: "This is like one great big faith family." We hoped that the transformation of the hall in Lac Brochet was a symbol of the rekindling of that "new life in a new community" that the people had originally envisioned for themselves.

Scripture

Be filled with the Spirit, as you sing psalms and hymns and spiritual songs among yourselves, singing and making melody to the Lord in your hearts, giving thanks to God the Father at all times and for everything in the name of our Lord Jesus Christ.

(Ephesians 5:18-20)

Prayer

Creator God and loving Father,
you form us into a holy people,
a nation set apart.
Grant us joy always in praising you together
and serving you in each other.
Bless our families, our communities and our world
with unity, harmony and peace.
This we ask through Christ our Lord. Amen.

The Church that Hugged

"Father, what are we going to do tomorrow?"

That question, coming close to midnight during a Deeper Search weekend for youth in the village of Pine House, brought my attention back to more practical matters.

All day Saturday, we had been caught up in a series of talks, prayer, small-group sharing and other activities for those who had already experienced a Search weekend and wanted some kind of follow-up. All had gone well for a first try, but now I realized we had never really decided what we would do Sunday.

After a quick discussion as a group, we arrived at a consensus. We wanted to share our weekend with the whole parish, so we would finish up at the Sunday liturgy, participating as fully as we could in the parish celebration. I would give a very brief homily and invite two Searchers to give a talk sharing their experience of Jesus through the Search movement. Hannah and

Dale Smith, who were brother and sister, responded quickly to the invitation and offered to give the talks.

The next morning, all the participants but one made it to the liturgy. When it was time for the homily, I set the context with a few brief comments, then Hannah got up to give her talk. I must admit to having some concerns, because I did not know how the community would accept their talks, nor could I be sure what the talks would be like or how long they might last.

"Why is it so hard to tell people that we love them?" Hannah began quietly. "One of the things we do at Search is to show our affection," she continued. "It is easy enough to do there. But my mother is dying of cancer and I want to tell her that I love her. However, every time I start to do that, the words get caught up in my throat and I can't do it." She then started to weep, and sat down to dry her tears.

I thought to myself, "Good, that was a great start, and short, too. This won't take too long." Then I watched as Dale got up to speak.

"People have funny ideas about Search," Dale began. "They think we talk about God all day and do nothing but pray. True, we do pray, but there is so much more. We talk about our lives and problems and share our feelings with one another, and as my sister was saying, even show our affection towards one another."

Suddenly, as Dale was talking, his friend Leonard got emotional, walked up to him without warning and gave him a hug. Dale graciously accepted the hug and continued unperturbed in his calm, quiet way.

"That's another thing I like about Search weekends," he stated. "We learn to hug and give each other hugs a lot. How come we don't do that in our families? We say that we are followers of Jesus and we come to church on Sunday but we don't show any affection at home. That can change and needs to change. What I want to do now is invite each of you to come up here and give me a hug. And if you don't want to or can't come up here to give me a hug, at least give a hug to the person next to you."

He then calmly stepped around the lectern and stood in front of it, waiting. I held my breath. "My God," I thought, "what is he doing? How will the people react to this?" There was a full minute of total silence. Then a woman stood up at the back of the church, marched right up to him, and gave him a hug. She was followed by another, then a teenager, then an older man, and suddenly the whole church was beginning to move, surging forward to give him a hug.

Someone had the presence of mind to nudge Hannah up beside him. Both stood there, calmly receiving hugs from young and old alike. It was just like a communion procession, only with a hug instead of a host.

I glanced at Sr. Alice LeStraat FDLP, the pastoral worker. She sat in her pew, almost beside herself with emotion, tears streaming down her face. Come to think of it, my face was damp with tears as well, so touching was this phenomenon of the whole church hugging these two young people with so much affection.

When the hugging had ended and Dale sat down, I started to compose myself to continue the liturgy, when Hannah appeared at the lectern again. She wanted to finish her talk. She began, "Another person I haven't been able to tell I love him is my dad. He's here today and if I can tell him, then maybe it will be easier to tell my mother. I want to ask my father to come up and give me a hug and I want to tell him that I love him."

There was another moment of suspenseful silence. Then James, a retired fisherman and recovering alcoholic, came right up to his daughter and gave her a great big, long bear hug. And as he wrapped his arms around her and cried on her shoulder, she sobbed in his ear those priceless words: "Dad, I love you."

That did it for me and for Sr. Alice. I, who find it hard to shed a tear, was crying unabashedly. Sr. Alice was having a hard time staying on her chair, so abundant were her tears. We continued the liturgy as best we could with a flood of emotions that remains impossible to describe. What we had witnessed had touched me – and, indeed, all of us – so deeply that the rest of the celebration seemed like a dream.

After the Eucharist, that euphoria of well-being stayed with me for a long time. I waved with love at everyone I saw as I drove around the village later on my way out. I felt a deep mellowness, not only in my heart but in my whole body as the community receded behind me.

Nothing else seemed to matter. All my other concerns and problems faded into pale insignificance. God was so real, love was present and the reign of God was growing right here, right now. All was well with the world. It was as if God had reached out and touched us, and we in turn had touched God, during that celebration in the church that hugged.

Scripture

Little children, let us love, not in word or speech, but in truth and action. ... if we love one another, God lives in us, and his love is perfected in us.

(1 John 3:18; 4:12)

Prayer

Creator God, loving Higher Power,
you who father and mother us,
yours is an unconditional love for us.
You accept us as we are and believe in who we can become.
Help us believe in the depth of your unconditional love for us
and let that love flow through us to others
in ways and words that will convey life and healing to them. Amen.

The Girl from Montreal Lake

The dull explosion thudded through the pine forest and sped up my steps towards the community.

There, a painful lesson not to judge others was seared into my soul forever.

It was a beautiful, calm, sunny afternoon in Beauval, perfect for a short jog to get some exercise. I changed into my jogging suit and headed towards a curving, sandy road up to Alex Burnouf's farm along the scenic Beaver River.

Some days earlier, a woman who was struggling with an abusive, alcoholic husband had visited me in the rectory, feeling very sad and discouraged. On impulse, I decided to drop in for a brief visit as I passed by her place.

As soon as I entered the door, I knew there was trouble. A drinking party was in full swing. Angry and upset, though undeterred, I resolved to accomplish the purpose for my visit. I made my way to the kitchen and found the woman there, trying to make the best of the situation.

As I was talking to her amid the din and clamour, I noticed a woman I didn't know sitting in a corner. When I asked who she was, I was told that she was a girl from Montreal Lake who had recently arrived in the village and was living with one of the local fellows and partygoers.

My generalized anger at everyone there suddenly had a focus. We had enough problems here without someone coming from elsewhere to create more. I felt my anger and resentment towards her quickly grow, piling up on what was already there.

Realizing that little could be accomplished in such a situation, I decided to leave and continue my jog as best as I could. The stranger had changed places, however, and was now standing in the hallway at the entrance to the house. I had to go right past her on my way out. I was tempted to ignore her, but on impulse made myself stop to chat with her, introduced myself and got to know her a bit.

It turned out that she had grown up in an abusive, alcoholic home. She had stayed with someone who had abused her for years, even to the point of locking her in a car trunk for hours. She finally had enough and escaped to Beauval, where she had some friends. My heart softened and I tried to be as sympathetic as I could. As we parted, she asked where I lived and if she could come to visit later that night after she sobered up. I agreed and left to continue jogging.

It was not easy to jog lightly with a heavy heart, so I did not go as far as I usually did. Or perhaps I wanted to free up the evening for the promised visit of this stranger. At any rate, I had turned around and was approaching the village when I heard an explosion.

I picked up my pace. As I emerged from the trees, I saw a column of black smoke spiralling into the sky. Racing into the village, I found a house on fire, flames pouring out of the windows and people scurrying around trying to organize a water brigade. "Was anyone still in the house?" I asked fearfully, my heart pounding and dreading the worst. I was told that the furnace had exploded without warning and that the family upstairs had made it out. However, there was someone downstairs, a girl from Montreal Lake. She was unable to get out and every attempt to save her had failed due to the fierce flames.

Later that night, Jules Roy came over to confirm my worst fears. They had recovered what was left of the body from the smouldering rubble of the house, which was totally destroyed. It was indeed the girl from Montreal Lake. Apparently she had left the party shortly after I left the house, presumably to go to where she was staying to sleep off the effects of the alcohol and, I would guess, get ready for our visit that evening. This decision led to the loss of her life in the fire that happened shortly after.

As reality sank in, I experienced a range of emotions: guilt that it was perhaps because of me that she had gone to that place at that time, anger, confusion, grief and sadness, all rolled into one.

It took a long time for these painful feelings to subside and for my thoughts to clear. I wondered at the mystery of such seemingly incomprehensible coincidences in life. Had I not stopped to visit, she probably would have not been in the house when it exploded. At the same time I felt gratitude for the short yet significant conversation we had had.

Who knows what she went through in that short period of time between one house and the next, between the drinking party and her attempt to sober up, and especially between our conversation and her death in that fire? Perhaps some hope was born, some resolve to change, some faith in a new start.

One thing I do know is that I learned a lesson that I will never forget. Each person carries within them their own mystery, which must be respected. I must strive to get to know a person rather than judge that person. That life lesson was seared into my being by that chance encounter with the girl from Montreal Lake.

Scripture

"Do not judge, so that you may not be judged. For with the judgement you make you will be judged, and the measure you give will be the measure you get. Why do you see the speck in your neighbour's eye, but do not notice the log in your own eye? You hypocrite, first take the log out of your own eye, and then you will see clearly to take the speck out of your neighbour's eye."

(Matthew 7:1-3, 5)

Prayer

Lord, you and you alone know the secrets of our hearts.
Only your Spirit plumbs the depths of our being.
You teach us that each person carries within them
a mystery that must be respected.
Grant us the awareness to see ourselves as we are
and our need to change first,
then the compassion to gently help others in their process of healing. Amen.

The Power of Fellowship

It took me three weeks to work up the courage and join the AA group, but I'm glad I did.

Join a support group and experience the power of fellowship.

During my first year of ministry in Beauval as a young missionary Oblate priest, I took life and ministry very seriously. After all, I was responsible for these people, and that responsibility weighed on me.

Another factor was that God didn't seem to be doing very much, so I determined that it was up to me to solve everyone's problems and change things for the better. I started working longer and longer hours, with almost no time for rest or relaxation. Everything became work, and life started getting to me. I felt like quitting the priesthood.

At the same time, I was attending local AA meetings as the pastor and would give a little spiritual talk at the end of each meeting. As time went on, this practice became ridiculous. The people were obviously happier than I was, so what could I offer them? In fact, they had something that I lacked and wanted.

I talked to the chairperson about joining the group, which meant I would have to share who I was and my feelings rather than give an intellectual talk. He supported me, saying that some people use the program even if they are not alcoholics.

I was afraid the people would reject me as their priest if I was honest and opened up about my personal situation. At the seminary I had shared the story of my life with my spiritual director, but never with a group of people that I knew like this.

Something inside me, however, kept pushing me to join. Aware of that gentle yet firm inner urging, when asked to speak about three weeks later, I responded by saying that I was joining the group. I shared my feelings and what I was going through at the time. My hands were sweating, my knees were shaking and I dared not look at anyone as I spoke.

When I had finished speaking, we stood and closed with the Lord's Prayer. After that prayer I stayed frozen in my place, eyes down, afraid to move. Then someone came up and shook my hand. Someone else gently placed a cup of coffee in my hand.

Suddenly there surged within me a feeling of belonging and acceptance that was one of the most powerful feelings of my life. I felt like I had come home, that I belonged. I was surrounded by people who were suddenly friends and not just parishioners, and I gratefully soaked up this new-found fellowship that memorable night.

Reflecting on that experience helped me understand the power of fellowship as love. For St. Paul, in 1 Corinthians 13:4-9, love is especially trust and acceptance. I had taken a risk. I had trusted these people and they had sensed my trust. They had listened to my pain and had taken my feelings into their hearts with deep respect. They had accepted me as I was.

Without understanding it fully, I had just experienced a powerful dose of love as trust and acceptance. That was a turning point for me in my ministry to the people of the north, leading to a whole new stage of personal growth for me as a person. I began to work the 12 Steps for myself. A few months after joining the program, I was asked to speak on spirituality at the Northwest Drug and Alcohol Rehabilitation centre in Île-à-la-Crosse. With the help of the staff and through the questions and experiences of the residents, I began to learn much about addictions and recovery. I began to see life and ministry with different eyes. I am still grateful for that experience, which colours my ministry to this day.

An insight expressed by Jean Vanier, founder of the L'Arche movement for people with developmental disabilities, helped me understand what happened that night. In a talk he gave in Edmonton in 1974, during my last year at the seminary, he stated simply, "When we are humble, honest and open enough to share our weakness with our brothers and sisters that frees them to be humble, honest and open enough to share their weakness with us and together we grow."

We were humble and honest that night. We opened up and shared our weaknesses with one another and together we grew and continue to grow. I cannot help but think that the small Coda group that met weekly for a year in one of our Oblate residences in the diocese of Prince Albert was a direct descendent of that small but significant AA support group in Beauval, which continues to this day.

So if you want to grow personally and experience a lot of healing love, join a support group.

Scripture

"Again, truly I tell you, if two of you agree on earth about anything you ask, it will be done for you by my Father in heaven. For where two or three are gathered in my name, I am there among them."
(Matthew 18:19-20)

Prayer

Lord, we believe in you.
Help us to believe in one another.
Strengthen not only our faith in you
but also our faith in each other.
Help us to realize that we come to you through one another.
Grant that we might put flesh to your inner spirit of love
by our trust in and our acceptance of others as they are.
Grant us new life through faith and fellowship. Amen.

A Christopher Couple

From north to south, from east to west. These four directions neatly sum up the life and ministry of the 1992 St. Joseph Award recipients.

The Catholic Church Extension Society (now Catholic Missions in Canada) is an organization that raises funds for and promotes home missions within Canada. Each year, the group honours someone who has been exemplary in living their faith commitment in a local church. In 1992, that award went to a couple, Ed and Angie Mihalicz. Hailing from southern Saskatchewan, they journeyed as newlyweds over 800 kilometres north in 1969 to be community teachers in Dillon, Saskatchewan.

So what did those years in between that journey north and receiving the award entail? That is quite a story. Not surprisingly, it involves a lot of travelling.

Back in the 1950s, being a community teacher in a northern Dené community meant being on call as teacher, pastor, nurse and policeman all wrapped into one. Ed and Angie recall being expected by the local Oblate missionary to put a stop to drinking parties and gambling events, among other duties.

After one year at Dillon, they taught two years on a southern reservation near Fort Qu'Appelle, followed by one more year in southern Alberta. By this time, the call to return to the north became irresistible. Responding to that call, they moved to Beauval, where Ed took a teaching position at the Beauval Indian Residential School and Angie focused on raising their five daughters. When the youngest, Michelle, began school, Angie returned to teaching. By then, Ed had taken on the additional duty of school principal.

In 1975, Ed and Angie were participants in the first Christopher Leadership Course to be offered in the north. They went on to become Christopher instructors, and helped spread the course to neighbouring communities. One such community was Patuanak. Introducing the course there meant midweek 100-kilometre trips at night, often in -30° winter weather, followed by three hours of preparation, teaching, evaluating and planning. They would arrive back home at midnight, ready to teach school the next day.

Involvement with the Christophers also meant, among other things, annual 1,400-kilometre round trips to Edmonton for the Instructors' seminar on a weekend, returning home at midnight and again teaching the next day. Ed's love for teaching the course earned him the nickname "Mr. Christopher."

It was also through the Christopher Course that they really got to know personally some of the people they had been working with at the residence for years. In a real sense, they moved from being teachers to being an integral part of the north. That subtle change was radically expressed when they purchased a lot in the community and built a house there. The north had truly become their home.

Little by little, they became very involved in local parish life. Angie played the organ both at the residence chapel and in the church in the community. She encouraged local musicians to play at church, teaching young Nicky Daigneault to play the organ so well that eventually he replaced her. She also started the Christian Ethics program at the residential high school. Part of that work included adapting a course called *Understanding the Bible* to include Aboriginal legends and spirituality. For one student from a southern reserve, the course became an RCIA experience. She became a believer and follower of Jesus and was able to share her witness at a Deeper Search weekend.

An important part of Angie's Grade 9 English class was to invite the students to write their autobiographies. She then graded what they wrote with a Christopher method of evaluation that was very affirming. In that way she got to know the students and was able to help guide many through their personal problems.

For his part, Ed became the first bulletin editor for the local parish and trained others in that role. He took on much of the administrative work for all the pastors and pastoral agents of that area during a few years of what was then called "Inter-Parish

Ministry." He also helped lead the community service in the absence of a priest and was instrumental in getting that practice started in Beauval. Ed was the driving force that helped get the Search for Christian Maturity movement started in Beauval in 1981. From that beginning, he and Angie were involved in almost every Search weekend in the north.

After school was over in June 1985, Ed left teaching and took on inter-parish work full-time. In 1986, Ed and Angie's involvement increased to the point that they decided to let go of teaching for a time and joined me in forming the Keewatin Renewal Team, at the request of then Archbishop Peter Sutton OMI. The basic thrust of this team was to offer Parish Renewals, Search weekends and Christopher Leadership Courses to all the communities within the archdiocese. We also tried to respond to other needs by putting on a communications workshop, hosting an Adult Children of Alcoholics session in Île-à-la-Crosse and Beauval, and getting involved with other events, such as the Sacred Circle Youth Camp and the Faith Family Festival.

The Parish Renewal experience was adapted from Chuck Gallagher's weekend experience. With the help of Fr. John Zunti OMI, we changed it from a weekend program to one that began on Sunday and was spread out over five nights. It involved gathering, singing and fellowship, scripture proclamation and teaching, talks and sharing in both small and large groups. The focus was on faith education and personal and communal healing. Sometimes the sessions went past midnight.

Our Parish Renewal ministry began in Sandy Bay, Saskatchewan, courtesy of Fr. Albert Ulrich OMI, who invited us for what turned out to be a very successful initiation of our program. It was almost overwhelming, both in terms of numbers of participants and their response to the process.

The years from 1987 to 1990 were full of activity for the team. After travelling north from the south as young teachers, Ed and Angie were now travelling east and west across the large expanse of the Keewatin-The Pas Archdiocese. The furthest point west was Yukon College in Whitehorse, where the team gave a Christopher Course and Instructors' Seminar back-to-back to students from across the Yukon. A rich part of that experience was meeting the late Bishop Tom Lobsinger OMI, who offered us his car to travel through Haines Junction over White Pass to Skakway, Alaska and back to Whitehorse.

The furthest point east was Sandy Lake, Ontario, where we offered the Christopher Course, experienced a unique graduation ceremony blended with local faith tradition, and participated in the blessing of the cornerstone for the new church. Meeting and getting to know Sidney and Harriet Fiddler, local lay leaders, was an enriching part of that eastern swing.

Through all this activity, the personal qualities of Ed and Angie shone like bright sunshine. Their faith, patience, understanding of First Nations spirituality and the northern people, teaching and administrative gifts, hospitality, love for God, the Church and God's people, family closeness, gentleness and generosity, to name a few qualities, were always in evidence.

Those qualities were obvious to many others as well. In 1992 they received the St. Joseph's Award at a special ceremony in Toronto. Ed is now retired from teaching adult education. Angie and Ed continue to volunteer in the community. Their family remains an important part of their life, and in 1999 they celebrated their 40th wedding anniversary.

So after starting in the south, travelling north and doing much ministry to the east and west, they are more settled now, but their journey continues unabated – a journey that will always take them into new adventures and sharing of faith.

Ad multos annos, Ed and Angie. *Kâ wî miyo payinawaw! Marci tcho!*

Scripture

Now there are varieties of gifts, but the same Spirit; and there are varieties of services, but the same Lord; and there are varieties of activities, but it is the same God who activates all of them in everyone. To each is given the manifestation of the Spirit for the common good.

(1 Corinthians 12:4-7)

Prayer

Lord, you came to live among us as one who serves,
not one who expected to be served.
That spirit of service led you to accept the cross
and give your life for us.
Help us to realize that our baptism is a commitment
to follow you in a life of service,
joyfully spending ourselves
and the gifts and talents you have given to us
to build up your Body the Church
and to help realize your reign here on earth. Amen.

Virginia's Dream

A dream, a Search weekend, a journey, a dream ... and finally, healing.

From a Beauval Search weekend that she attended with her son in 1985, to the present day, Virginia has had a remarkable healing journey.

As mentioned earlier, one of the goals of a Search week-end is to increase the level of communication between parents and their teenage sons and daughters. Virginia returned to the next Search weekend with her husband, and later that same year attended a third weekend with her daughter. She then participated in many other faith events, such as the Christopher Leadership Course, pilgrimages, Marriage Encounter, Faith Family Festivals and, finally, Cursillo.

Interwoven with all these personal and communal growth events were countless letters and phone conversations. Slowly but surely, her story started to emerge: first, her struggle with her marriage and her family, then, little by little, her past as a young girl growing up in northern Saskatchewan.

Her teenage dream was to be a woman religious, a sister. As a step towards realizing that dream, she had left her community for one year to attend a special boarding school. Back home for the summer, her dream was suddenly shattered when a teenage neighbour sexually molested her.

That incident started a downward spiral for her. She tried to share her pain with her mother, who blamed and scolded her. The police at that time did not take her seriously. She felt shamed and dirty and judged herself unworthy to be a sister. She was afraid to tell the truth to the local parish priest, who had supported her dream of being a nun. Confused and heart-broken, she gave up on her dream.

She then left home, hurting and angry at her abuser, at God and at her mother, who died a few years later. Feeling guilty for the unresolved situation with her mother, she developed an ulcer. Within months, she started to drink as a way to cope with her pain.

Eventually, Virginia married and had four children, two boys and two girls. The pain was always with her, however, so she turned to the use of alcohol and prescription drugs to medicate that pain. Even when she was pregnant, she drank. Her marriage was strained and communication with her husband and children reached a very low level.

Virginia's first step towards healing was to tell her story. That took time – much time – but eventually the story came out. At the same time, her faith deepened. She began to see how God was at work in her life. She learned that God does not prevent suffering, but rather, God *shares* our suffering. She realized that Jesus, the Messiah who suffered for us, was there with her when she was sexually abused and that through her, he was also sexually abused. She learned that he would now help her to handle her abuse as he handled his abuse, through forgiveness and loving his enemies.

Forgive and love her abuser? That was impossible for her, but not for God. Finally, she turned to the Lord in faith and surrender and became willing to follow him through a healing process of learning how to forgive.

Matthew 18:15-17 came to life for her. In that passage, Jesus teaches his disciples how to love their enemies as a way of forgiving them: "If your brother does something wrong [*abuses you*], then go alone and point out his fault [*tell him how you feel*]."

Ironically, rehabilitation centres can be better at teaching this truth than the Church is. They coach their residents to use a formula of "I" statements, which runs like this: "When you [here the person describes the abusive actions of the other] ..., I felt/still feel" [here they describe their feelings and the impact those actions had on their life] ...."

The key to the success of this formula is to do it *with love*. There must be no judgment, revenge, vindication or punishment, but rather only communication with love. As one therapist put it, "To confront with expectation is manipulation." And manipulation does not heal; it may assuage anger but it creates more hurt and guilt. The challenge for those who are abused is to discipline themselves to communicate with love. That discipline in itself is love, and a great step towards forgiving by letting go of the hurt and anger.

That is what Virginia did. She wrote a letter to her abuser using that formula. It took about eleven attempts. She ripped up and threw away the first ten letters because in those she was acting out of anger, attacking and name calling, instead of just expressing her hurt and anger with love.

Finally, she had a letter she thought she would be able to send. She read it to me over the phone to check it out, then gave it to a friend, who delivered it personally to her abuser. Part of her growth in love was the desire to avoid hurting his marriage and family. She knows he got the letter because a number left on her phone some days later showed that he tried to contact her.

That courageous action was a major turning point for her. She felt lighter and was set free to move on with her life, though not without some relapses, which continued to require attention.

She also needed to forgive herself, which was just as hard, because she blamed herself for the problems her children were having. A key step towards that self-forgiveness occurred when she was finally able to put into words exactly what happened to her the day of the abuse and share that with another trusted person. As she heard herself speaking those words and felt the acceptance of the other, she began to forgive herself.

A final step was the need to grieve. At the age of 45, married and a mother of four, she still wanted to be a nun. The dream she had given up on as a teenager was still with her, haunting her, nagging away at her. What could she do?

She began to work with a counsellor. She took a grief workshop and continued informal spiritual direction with me. At one such session, with her husband present, it struck me forcibly that her dream of being a nun was like a broken vase of glass. She was trying to carry that vase of shattered glass with her, cutting herself and bleeding her way through life.

As I mentioned that image to her, I asked her how she felt. Her response was to wordlessly grab her necklace and tear it apart, strewing pearls around the room. Obviously, the feeling was anger. Reasonable enough, I thought, given the depth of her loss. We talked some more until her feelings turned to, in her words, incredible sadness. That, too, made sense to me, for if she was trying to say goodbye to a dream, there would have to be some sadness.

At the end of that night of deep soul-work, her feelings were simply "emptiness." That had me stumped until the next day, when she shared with me a dream she had had during the night. In her dream, she was in a church. The sanctuary was empty and bare. There was no altar, only a picture of Jesus on the wall. She was kneeling on a black box praying her rosary when a whirlwind came and took the black box away. She stood up and was reaching for the box with her rosary in her hands when she awoke from the dream.

As I heard her share her dream, I felt great excitement. Knowing how important dreams are to the First Nations peoples and in the Bible, I have learned to take them seriously. She wasn't sure of the meaning of the dream so I shared my interpretation. To me the dream was a confirmation of her grieving and healing process of the past months, and especially the work of the previous night.

With growing faith in the Lord who had suffered for, with and through her, she had allowed him to take her back into her past with faith, represented by the rosary. She allowed him to touch her wounds and heal her hurt and anger with forgiveness. Now he was healing her of her self-pity and the grief of her loss. The church sanctuary without an altar was where she left off the night before, feeling empty. She had to go there, into that emptiness, with faith. There she would find the Lord, represented by the picture on the wall.

Virginia had always tried to escape the pain of her loss and emptiness in the past through alcohol, drugs and other destructive activities. Now, with faith, she had turned around, gone into that pain and found Jesus waiting for her there. She had grieved and expressed her anger, sadness and emptiness, and was now ready to let go and give it to God. So the Holy Spirit in the whirlwind came to free her from her shattered dream, which had turned into a coffin, the black box she was trying to drag through life.

That dream was a turning point for her. It turned out to be a liberating dream that helped to heal her of her frustrated dream of being a sister. She was ready to move on now, and move on she did. Later that summer she accepted to be the rectora for a Cursillo that was held in northern Saskatchewan. Being rectora was a very demanding responsibility, but she was ready and did it well. She is also helping others deal with similar issues in their lives.

Virginia's story stands out for me as an inspiring example of a woman who, in the midst of life's hurt, dared to act on faith and discovered the healing power of fellowship and self-awareness.

It also reminds me of the very gentle, incarnate way that our loving God works in our lives. Through dreams, prayer and community, our compassionate God seeks to heal us and restore us to new life if we will but trust his Son and follow him through the Paschal mystery that is our own healing journey.

Scripture

Now to him who by the power at work within us is able to accomplish abundantly far more than all we can ask or imagine, to him be glory in the church and in Christ Jesus to all generations, for ever and ever. Amen.

(Ephesians 3:20-21)

Prayer

Creator God and loving Father,
you sent your only Son as the Messiah
who suffered and died out of love for us.
As the faithful One,
he transformed that death into new life through forgiveness.
Give us the faith and courage to follow him into our own Paschal mystery,
letting him touch our wounds with forgiveness and healing,
so that we might rise with him to a new life of serenity and joy. Amen.

Visiting Mary

Redemptive suffering: two words that simply and starkly describe Mary's life.

Years after her death, the memory of her cheerfulness in the midst of physical and personal pain still fills me with awe. The desire to imitate her in transcending my own limitations and difficulties stirs deep within me.

Mary Jacobson was a simple, ordinary yet extraordinary elderly woman living alone in Île-à-la-Crosse. She was one of the homebound elders I would visit regularly as pastor. Her house was a very humble dwelling in the northern part of the community overlooking the lake.

To enter her home was an experience in itself. Her cheerful greeting would float out as a faint voice from the bedroom. Mary was bedridden with crippling rheumatoid arthritis that had deformed her back and gnarled her hands but had not in any way dampened her spirit.

As one entered her bedroom, she would already be involved in the difficult process of raising herself to a sitting position on her bed, or manoeuvring herself onto her wheelchair with the help of a vertical pole near the bed. As usual, she would be chuckling and laughing to herself as she did so.

Her bedroom was a cozy, cluttered, comfortable nook. More accurately, it was her home and living space. Holy pictures, family pictures, candles and religious articles abounded. And always, her rosary was in her hand. Mary was one of the most prayerful people I have ever met. Her days were mostly days of prayer into which she would insert other activities.

She delighted in receiving visitors and especially in receiving communion. She exuded warmth, cheerfulness, joy, peace and hospitality. From the moment a visitor arrived, her room was filled with smiles, laughter, good-natured banter and pleasant conversation about life, the community, her family, God, the saints, Mary, the Church, prayer and the latest person to end up in some kind of difficulty for whom she was praying.

One of those persons would invariably be one of her sons, whom she would be literally praying into sobriety. Martin was one such son. After several unsuccessful sessions of treatment in various rehabilitation centres, he seemed to be a hopeless case. Mary never gave up hope, however, and kept on praying for him. He sobered up eventually and became the director of the North West Drug and Alcohol Rehabilitation centre in Île-à-la-Crosse.

As I arrived for a visit, the table was prepared and candles were lit. Mary would begin singing one of her favourite Cree hymns from her weathered old hymn book, and we would pray part of her beloved rosary. A reading from the scriptures would follow, interspersed with a dialogue commentary and prayers for those in need. Finally, the moment for communion would come and we would be caught up in her joy at this moment of sacramental intimacy with her Lord.

After a moment of reverent silence, she would want to sing all eight verses of a Cree thanksgiving hymn. Then we would say the closing prayer, followed by the blessing. After that, there would be more laughter, visiting and perhaps a cup of tea that she had prepared herself, never counting the cost in terms of personal effort. Nothing was too good for her guests. She would use her walker and hobble around as best she could, chattering cheerfully all the time.

Leaving was always a difficult moment. It was hard to leave because it was such a pleasure to be in her presence and spend time with her. Never have I seen so much joyful suffering in one person. What a gift she was to all who knew her. What an inspiring, unsung example for us all.

And what joy it is to be writing these details about her and in this small way sing her praises to those who never had the blessing of meeting her. Maybe in this way, the reader can also visit with Mary a little and be touched by her spirit of joyful, redemptive suffering.

Scripture

*The end of all things is near; therefore be serious and discipline yourselves
for the sake of your prayers. Above all, maintain constant love for one
another, for love covers a multitude of sins. Be hospitable to one another
without complaining. Like good stewards of the manifold grace of God,
serve one another with whatever gift each of you has received. ... whoever
serves must do so with the strength that God supplies, so that God may be
glorified in all things through Jesus Christ. To him belong the glory and
the power for ever and ever.*

(1 Peter 4:7-10, 11b)

Prayer

*Lord, we thank you for putting into our lives
friends and elders who inspire us by their faith
and mirror for us your compassion and long-suffering love.
Grant that we may also consider any suffering in the present
as nothing compared to the glory you promise us.
Give us only the strength to find you in our difficulties
and receive your strength to overcome them with cheerful patience. Amen.*

A Tale of Three Communities

What is the difference between being addicted to alcohol and being addicted to bingo?

People who are addicted to bingo remember their last blackout!

In 1988, our Keewatin Renewal Team was invited by the three communities of Canoe Narrows, Jans Bay and Cole Bay, Saskatchewan, to come and give a Parish Renewal in Canoe Narrows, an hour's drive north of Meadow Lake. We were open to going on the condition that there would be no bingos at the same time. The local leaders agreed and shut down bingos in the hall and on the local TV for the week.

The Renewal always began with a half-hour of gathering that consisted of singing, visiting and telling jokes. The goal of the renewal was above all to strengthen the faith of the people.

This particular renewal went very well, with about a hundred people of all ages coming nightly to take in this faith-building and community-healing event.

To accommodate the elders, who were more fluent in Cree, Eugene Yew served as a translator. He did well until he got tired and started to repeat in English what had just been said in English, to everyone's amusement.

The principal of the school at that time, Ron Skage, shared with me years later that he noticed a difference in the community for at least a whole year after the Parish Renewal, and wanted the same experience for the other community where he was working.

My first introduction to Canoe Narrows was in Île-à-la-Crosse, where I was spending the summer as a scholastic. One night I was called to the deathbed of John Iron, the former chief of Canoe Narrows. I arrived to find the hospital room packed with family, relatives and friends.

We prayed the rosary interspersed with Cree hymns. As John breathed his last, I was able to share some prayers for the dying and then prayers after the moment of death. The atmosphere in the room was one of tangible faith. We could almost see his soul being lifted up to heaven on the wings of prayer. Though there was grief, sorrow and crying, there was also a profound peace and even joy at such a beautiful death. It was a touching experience for a young Oblate scholastic – one that I will always remember.

Some years later, as a newly ordained priest stationed in Beauval, I offered to replace the elderly Fr. Eduoard Perreault

OMI, pastor of Canoe Narrows, Cole Bay and Jans Bay. He loved to travel and wanted to take a month's holiday with Fr. Lemay OMI of Buffalo Narrows. Fr. Perreault was a dapper individual who always dressed in a suit and loved to play cribbage.

Staying in the little rectory in Canoe Narrows by the lake was my holiday that year. I studied the encyclical *Evangelization of the Modern World* by Pope Paul VI in the morning, swam and sunned myself in the afternoon, and played slow pitch with the youth during the long summer evenings. I was struck by the friendliness and helpfulness of the people, not to mention the involvement of men in the Church.

One of those men was the late Senator Jonas Larivière, who lived to be over a hundred years old. Up to the time of his death, he lived on his own, close to his son and his family. He was a man of deep, simple faith. Though he was one of the saintliest persons I knew, he invariably humbly requested to celebrate the sacrament of reconciliation whenever a priest visited the community, an experience that never failed to leave me edified.

Jonas was a genuine pilgrim. He had been to Guadalupe in Mexico many times, as well as overseas, and made an annual pilgrimage to Lac Ste. Anne in Alberta. He travelled 700 kilometres to my ordination as an archbishop, and was one of the elders who gathered around to bless me as part of that moving ceremony. The next day, just before leaving to return home, he stopped by to visit. Moved by that gesture, I asked him to bless me again. He placed his hands on my head and prayed a blessing in his own Cree language. I felt as Jesus might have felt when the Father spoke from the heavens to bless him after he was baptized in the Jordan.

Canoe Narrows was the site for a memorable experience for me as a young priest. Solomon and Philomene Iron were celebrating their 75th wedding anniversary and I had the honour of presiding at that celebration. Solomon was 97 years old and Philomene 93. Greetings came from the Queen and then Prime Minister Pierre Elliott Trudeau, along with a papal blessing from the Vatican. Both Solomon and Philomene were alert, sitting in wheel chairs during the ceremony. At one point, Solomon reached up and tried to take the papal blessing from me as I read it out, claiming that it was his: *"Niya anima obci."* They were later joined at the banquet by their good friend, 100-year-old John Corrigal. Given the shifting sands around the whole question of marriage in our day, what role models these two elders were as a couple for us all.

On weekends I would make the fifteen-minute journey to Cole Bay, a small resort settlement on the south side of the lake. One day, I decided I would walk there for exercise. I had no sooner set out than a young fellow pulled up beside me to give me a ride. His parents had noticed me walking and sent him to take me there. So much for my walk!

Cole Bay was notable for three elders: the late Alex Desjarlais, Dan McCallum and the late Victor Couillonneur. They would often sit on the grass in the churchyard in the summer, discussing what they could do for the Church. From that planning came a beautiful grotto built by the people of

Cole Bay that expressed their faith and was blessed by the late Archbishop Paul Dumouchel OMI. It was the site of many pilgrimages and even the profession of final vows by one of our former Oblates.

I remember mentioning to the parish pastoral council gathering one evening that the outdoor toilets were full, but in my broken Cree this message came out as "the toilets had eaten enough." A month later, I noticed that new holes had been dug, and the toilets moved. I commented in my fledgling Cree at the meeting that night that the toilets were now "hungry," to the amusement of all.

At the same meeting, I asked what other needs the parish had. Victor replied that they needed new mops for the church. I was hoping for a more substantial contribution, but that was a start. It was the same Victor who told the RCMP when they stopped to check on him by his stalled car that the battery had "passed away."

Jans Bay is a small community at the other end of the lake, past the narrows. The people of Jans Bay are unique, in that even though there was a church a few miles away and no priest was assigned to the village, they took the initiative and built a small log chapel for themselves, completely on their own. I had the opportunity to bless that chapel, which was heated by a wood stove.

One summer in Jans Bay, a hide-tanning course was offered. Curious, I stopped by to learn more about the process. When I asked what was used to soften the hide, Hermaline Gardiner innocently replied, "The brains of the animal, but if you don't have any brains, Father, then you would use bear grease." Those standing nearby who caught on to the unintended innuendo enjoyed her comment. It was also in Jans Bay that I had my first experience as a disk jockey, spending an hour or so playing hymns on the local radio and sharing a faith commentary.

This story of three communities began on a note of faith, and I want to end it on the same note. One year, a young man in Canoe Narrows committed suicide. The family, devastated by the tragedy, was supported by the strong faith and love of the community and the whole area. There was much traditional and gospel singing and praying of the rosary, as well as visiting and comforting of the family throughout the wake, the funeral and afterwards.

I believe it is in Canoe Narrows that the idea of a memorial prayer service for those who died developed. One was held for the family a year later. When I went to the community for a thanksgiving mass after my episcopal ordination, I was invited by the family to their home, where they had built a closed-in gazebo over the spot where the death had occurred.

Inside the gazebo was a small shrine where remnants of their son's body were found and buried. Young people now gather there in the evenings for a time of remembering, prayer and sharing. It is a healing gazebo, a place to grow stronger in faith so that such things never happen again. Lives are being touched and transformed by this gazebo. Grief has been turned into good grieving and a source of hope. It is a shelter that faith has built and where faith can grow stronger.

As I left Canoe Narrows that evening and passed by Jans Bay, I marvelled at the human spirit, which can turn sadness into peace and despair into hope. I was reminded once again of the importance of being a faith-filled person by these three faith-filled communities.

Scripture

Now faith is the assurance of things hoped for, the conviction of things not seen. Indeed, by faith our ancestors received approval. By faith we understand that the worlds were prepared by the word of God, so that what is seen was made from things that are not visible.

(Hebrews 11:1-3)

Prayer

Creator God and loving Father,
you called the Hebrew people out of Egypt in a great act of liberation,
and formed them into your people by the gift of your Word in the desert.
Grant that our communities today may be places of healing,
freedom and wholeness for all,
as we continue to be formed by your Word into a holy nation,
a people set apart to proclaim your love. Amen.

A Harvest of Reconcilation

Some call it a sixth sense. Whatever it is called, I am sure it was at work when I first met, or rather saw, Ernie. It was my first week of ministry in the community, and I was going door to door introducing myself to everyone as well as practising my Cree.

As I approached this one house, I noticed two men bent over the grille of an old car some distance away, obviously trying to repair something. As I neared the steps, I had the strange feeling that they were aware of my approach but pretended not to notice. I hesitated. Should I disturb them or should I continue up the steps and knock on the door? For some reason, I simply turned back and returned to my car, resolving to return another day.

A few weeks later, I returned to the same house. This time, not seeing anyone in the yard, I went right up to the door and knocked. The door opened and there stood Ernie. "Great," I thought, "he is home, and we will visit." Not so. I had barely begun to greet him in Cree when he realized that I was the new priest. His eyes narrowed, his face darkened and suddenly there poured out of him a stream of profanity. Cursing and swearing, he told me to go run a residential school, as well as some unmentionable things I could do at that residential school.

I was shocked and made a vain attempt to find out why he was so angry, to no avail. Ernie started shouting, "Get the hell out of here!" I thought he was talking to the dogs that were around my legs but quickly saw that he was directing those words at me. Then he reached for something and I thought, "Oh my God, he is going for a gun!"

I quickly turned away, rushed down the steps and headed for the safety of my car. Glancing over my shoulder, I saw him standing on the steps, brandishing a hockey stick in my direction and continuing to utter profanities.

I started the engine and drove out of the yard as quickly as I safely could, driving straight across the road into the churchyard hidden in the bush. There I stopped, my heart pounding, my whole body shaking, while I recovered my breath.

It took a while for the intense feelings of fear and shock to dissipate. I felt weak and threatened. I just wanted to go home and stop any further visiting. I began to wonder what it was that could make a man so angry. Was he a victim of abuse at a residential school? How could he be helped? What should I do now?

Luckily, earlier that day I had been invited by one of the ladies more involved in the church to go to her home for supper and a memorial healing circle. I managed to visit a few more places, then made my way to her place. I chose not to say anything about the incident with Ernie, not being sure who he was or how he might be related to this family.

After supper, we went to the living room, placed a quilt on the floor, with a candle in the centre, and sat around for an hour of prayer and sharing about this woman's mother, who had died a year earlier. Unknown to this family, that beautiful, peaceful candlelight session was just what I needed to revive my battered and bruised spirit. I resolved to find some way to bring healing to the abusive man I had just encountered.

Discreetly, I asked around about him. I learned that he was abusive and had quite a reputation. A year went by as I wondered who could go with me to visit him in a safe way. Then, in an adjacent community, I met a woman who told me that he was her uncle and that yes, he was known to be very abusive. I asked her if she could go with me to visit him someday, and she agreed.

Before that could happen, however, she told me that he was hospitalized in another province and had been diagnosed with cancer. I decided that the next time I was in that city, I would go to see him, alone if I had to.

Some months later, I discovered that Ernie was back home in the palliative care unit of the local hospital dying of cancer, and that he might not have much more time to live. Then and there I resolved to visit him as soon as I could.

That day finally came. I could not help but feel that same fear and trepidation as I approached his room. What if he was still angry and lashed out at me again? I summoned up my courage, said a prayer, and entered his room.

Ernie was lying on the bed talking on his cellphone. I was struck by how thin he was. He motioned with his hand to go around the bed and take a chair by the window. So far so good, I thought as I waited for him to finish talking on the phone. He did not seem angry now so I felt some hope that we might be able to at least visit a bit and uncover the reason for all that previous pent-up anger.

Ernie finally put away the phone and sat up a bit. We made small talk for a few minutes as he described when he got sick, his stay in the city and when he returned to the hospital here. I asked him what it was like to be that sick and what the diagnosis was.

Then I heard Ernie say that being sick had given him a lot of time to think. I wondered to myself if he remembered the incident when I dropped by his house some years earlier. He went on to say that he realized he had a lot of things to say he was sorry for. My heart almost stopped. Could that include the incident with me?

Almost immediately, in a quiet yet sincere voice, Ernie spoke the words I will never forget" "I am sorry for what I did to you that day, Father." A rush of love, surprise, gratitude and relief flooded my whole being, mixed with shock, for this was way more than I ever dared hope. I tried to control my feelings and, as calmly as I could, told him that yes, I had felt very afraid that day and ever since then had wanted to talk to him, to ask him, "Why so much anger?" Had he been abused as a student at the residential school?

He replied quite openly that no, he had not been abused, but he had lost all of his school buddies and friends who had attended the school with him. They were all gone. He went on to share that they had either died violently in fights, had committed suicide or drank themselves to death. He was angry at the whole system that had such a tragic impact on his people. That day I visited his house I became the lightning rod for his anger, as I represented the system to him.

I told Ernie that I understood and that I forgave him. I also extended an apology to him for any hurt that had happened to him and his friends directly or indirectly because of the residential school. He stretched out his hand and as we shook hands, our eyes met and my heart melted as I saw the pain but also the repentance and the forgiveness in his eyes. I wanted to shout for joy, and felt — what did I feel? Was it hope, joy, perhaps even love? Certainly this was a reconciliation that was tangible and touched every cell in my body, not to mention my spirit.

I made my way back towards the door, wanting to savour this moment and not impose on him in any way. Ernie began to talk some more, sharing how he wanted to do so much for the youth but now he couldn't. He asked me if I would take them to powwows and suggested that the church in his community needed to be fixed up. I could hardly believe my ears. Was this the same man who years earlier had driven me out of his yard with curses?

We shook hands again and I gave him a blessing. I was honest with him, telling him that I was scheduled to go to Kenya for a month, so this might be goodbye, but that I would continue to pray for him. His response was to grab my hand a third time and just hold it.

I drove home that day elated and profoundly moved. This was a kingdom moment. This man, so unchurched and previously so angry, was entering the kingdom of God through his simple apology and our reconciliation. This was amazing grace! This man was doing what so many other people who are more educated and privileged struggle to do. He was apologizing, asking for forgiveness, making amends and being reconciled with those whom he had hurt. It doesn't get any better than this.

As I flew across the ocean a few days later, I felt not only the thrust of the plane's engines that had carried us into the skies, but even more felt the buoyancy of the memory of that event that filled me with joy. That joy stayed with me all the way to my destination, Meru, Kenya, where I offered sessions on addictions awareness and leadership courses to the pre-novices.

At one point during my stay, Bro. Harley Mapes OMI, who was assisting the director, Fr. Bill Stang OMI, asked me if I would consider staying and working in Kenya, as there was such a harvest of vocations there. My response was to share the above story with him. I needed to stay home and work towards a harvest of reconciliation with the First Nations people, as difficult as that might be. It is a harvest that I had been privileged to experience in a powerful way through Ernie.

Scripture

So when you are offering your gift at the altar, if you remember that your brother or sister has something against you, leave your gift there before the altar and go; first be reconciled to your brother or sister, and then come and offer your gift.

(Matthew 5:23-24)

Prayer

Lord, help us to be in touch with our own inner reality.
If we are carrying anger, help us to move towards forgiveness.
If there is any guilt from something we have said, done or omitted to do,
give us the humility, faith and raw courage to freely admit it,
ask for forgiveness, and seek to make amends,
that we might be reconciled and live and die in your peace. Amen.

Speaking a New Language

How do you handle hurt in your life? Try communicating with love.

Violet had been raised by her grandparents. They gave her away at age thirteen to a man who wanted her as a wife for his son. The son, much older than she, turned out to be a very abusive, alcoholic partner. She stayed in the common-law relationship for as long as she could and had six children. At one point he threatened to kill her, brandishing a gun or a knife. Finally, after her children had grown and she was not able to take the abuse anymore, Violet left him for her own safety.

As time went on, she entered into another relationship with someone who was unfaithful and who eventually left her. Shortly after that, we met at her brother's home when I dropped in for a visit. She was crying and willingly reached out for help.

It was obvious that her first need was to heal from the scars of this last relationship, which left her feeling betrayed and abandoned. Through sharing with her brother and sister-in-law, as well as with what spiritual direction I could give her, she was able to start a healing journey, pick up the pieces and move on with her life.

At about that time, the Christopher Leadership Course was introduced in a nearby community. She registered for that first course, enjoyed it and grew in confidence and self-esteem.

Then came Cursillo. The Cursillo movement began in Spain during the last World War and subsequently spread to North America. The basic weekend experience is seen as a three-day walk with the Lord and a short course on Christianity, hence the name "Cursillo," which means "short course" in Spanish.

The Cursillo had a tremendous impact on Violet's life. There she learned more about her Christian Catholic faith and saw it put into action. She heard stories similar to hers. She was able to share much of her pain and heal some of her anger and resentment towards the men who had abused her so much. She went on to help with a subsequent weekend and was asked to give one of the talks.

With her faith appetite whetted, she began to worship regularly at her local church and was instrumental in helping form a sharing circle in her community that consisted of singing, scripture study, sharing of needs and prayer.

Her next step was to participate in a lay formation program called *Builders of a New Earth*, developed by the Jesuits in

South Dakota. Violet finished the first year of that course and grew stronger in her understanding of the gift of faith and the church.

Around this time, something happened that not only helped her test her new wings of faith, but also gave her an experience of the power of *agape* love, which Jesus taught and lived.

She was visiting her daughter in town one day when she answered the phone. It was her ex-partner and the father of her children. Thinking that he was talking to their daughter, he proceeded to unleash a furious attack on Violet, berating her and putting her down. Without comment, she hung up the phone and felt all the old anger, hurt and resentment reach a boiling point.

Formerly, such an incident would have thrown her into tears and deep confusion. Her recent involvement with the Church, however, had taught her to "communicate with love," based on the teachings of Jesus in Matthew 18:15 ("If another member of the church sins against you, go and point out the fault when the two of you are alone.") and Matthew 5:44 ("Love your enemies.") She had even learned that there was a formula to help her practice this key teaching. All she had to do was to remind her former partner of what he had done to her and share with him how she felt because of his behaviour, without any judgment or manipulation on her part. This was where the discipline of love came into play. There could be no revenge, no getting even or even name calling – just communication with love.

So instead of acting out of anger, she wrote him a letter describing what he had said and expressing her feelings of hurt and anger in a positive manner with love. When she phoned me to share what she had done, I encouraged her to do even more. To her credit, she summoned up her courage and decided to deliver the letter personally, rather than mail it. She travelled with her daughter to a nearby community to deliver the letter to him while he was attending a meeting.

Her daughter went into the meeting to get him while Violet waited in the truck outside. When he came up to the vehicle, she handed him the letter, saying, "I need to share something with you. It's all in the letter. Please read it." His reaction upon reading the letter was instant anger and another put-down. She replied calmly, "There is no need to argue. I just want to let you know how I feel about what just happened between us. It's all in the letter. Please read it again."

He did so, and this time his reaction was to stand there, open mouthed and speechless. Then he said simply, "Okay," turned around and returned to the meeting. Their daughter, who had watched apprehensively from her side of the truck, said with awe in her voice, "M-o-o-o-m!" She had never seen her mother relate to her father this way before. Previously, it had always been a fight. Returning home, Viola was filled with a profound, mysterious, exhilarating joy.

Sorting out her emotions afterwards over the phone with me, the import of what she had done came to me. She had loved her enemy, her own ex-partner who had just abused her. She had communicated with love. She had actually forgiven him of that incident in the process and was free from anger and resentment.

With growing excitement, I pointed out to her that she was experiencing the signs that Jesus told his disciples would accompany them: by using my name they will cast out demons; they will speak in new tongues; they will pick up snakes in their hands, and if they drink any deadly thing, it will not hurt them; they will lay their hands on the sick, and they will recover" (Mark 16:17-18).

Violet had taken up this potentially dangerous incident (the snake Jesus spoke of), had dealt with it positively (drank the deadly poison), and had used the language of love (spoken in a new tongue) so effectively that her daughter marvelled at her. She was casting out the demon of fear, and healing the relationship between her, her ex-partner and her daughter. In fact, years later, she was the one who cared for him as he lay dying of cancer. She was truly a disciple of Jesus who was experiencing the reign of God and the power of the resurrection in her life. The signs Jesus spoke of were accompanying her.

So if there is hurt in your life, don't act out of anger. Instead, choose to communicate with love, to speak a new language as a way of coming to forgiveness, and you also will experience that mysterious peace that only Jesus can give to those who truly learn to love.

Scripture

"If another member of the church sins against you, go and point out the fault when the two of you are alone. If the member listens to you, you have regained that one. But if you are not listened to, take one or two others along with you, so that every word may be confirmed by the evidence of two or three witnesses. If the member refuses to listen to them, tell it to the church; and if the offender refuses to listen even to the church, let such a one be to you as a Gentile and a tax-collector."

(Matthew 18:15-17)

Prayer

*Lord, you have shown us that the power of your love
is the power to forgive any hurt that has come our way.
Give us the humble faith and raw courage to feel our feelings,
ponder them, process them and express them with love to those
who have hurt us.
Help us to let go of fighting out of anger and fleeing out of fear.
Help us to move instead towards forgiveness through faith in you. Amen.*

An Impossible Healing Journey

I had lost track of her for many years after she and her family mysteriously moved to another community. Then one day, Rosita re-entered my life and ministry and solved the mystery with her plea for help.

That plea led us both to the experience of an impossible healing journey, a journey that only faith in Jesus and the power of genuine *agape* love could accomplish.

I first met Rosita in the northern community where she lived with her husband and children. It was hard not to notice her as she was so involved in the Church. Whether it was organizing events, initiating projects, over-seeing faith education, or being part of the first parish council, she was there. She was a driving force in her community and a natural leader. When she took on a commitment, she always carried it through. I began to depend on her for many aspects of the life of the Church in her community.

Fairly often, however, flashes of anger would break through Rosita's usually composed manner. There was a certain tension, sharpness, almost cynical tone to the way she carried out her ministry and her family life. A few times, when unaware of my approach to her house, I would overhear angry outbursts from her that she would never have demonstrated in my presence.

I wondered what could be the reason for this apparent dichotomy in Rosita's life. She was a puzzle to me. How could a person have so much faith and be so dedicated and involved, yet carry such an angry edge within her? The answer to that mystery came years later when, along with a plea for help, she shared her story.

What I did not know when I first met Rosita and observed her leadership skills (and her suppressed anger) was that she was a victim of sexual abuse. A relative in an adjacent community had raped her twice when she was fourteen years old. He threatened her so she was afraid to tell anyone.

Rosita carried that shame, confusion and anger into her adult years, and started to abuse alcohol as a way of numbing her pain. Then she fell in love with and married a relative of her abuser. They lived in the same small community, where she saw her abuser almost every day. The ever-present pain led her to continue to abuse alcohol, even when she was pregnant with her children.

After many years of that strained existence, Rosita realized that she could not continue to drink, and managed to stop. The pain was still there, however, so she turned to another addiction: playing bingo and gambling. Added to this personal pain was the conflict within her of her double life. She felt guilty about the contradiction between her faith in God and her love for the Church and her family on the one hand, and her addictions on the other.

One day, her abuser's son molested her 13-year-old daughter. That was it. Rosita moved back to her home community with her husband and family. That was when I lost track of her, as she had moved outside of the archdiocese in which I was ministering. I heard rumours of abuse, but was never able to get the whole story.

Years passed, then one day her own son molested her granddaughter, one of the girls of her own daughter who had been abused. She reacted strongly, informing the police of what her son had done. Her action led to him being put into a correctional facility for youth.

Then Rosita fell apart. This latest incident brought back the memory of the abuse that she had suffered as a teenager. She realized that she had never really dealt with her experience. She had only buried it, and now that abuse was repeating itself generationally. There were now three generations of sexual abuse in her family. She knew it was time to do something. That was when she reached out and called me for help.

We decided it was time for her to embark on a 12 Step healing journey. She admitted that she was powerless over the effects of sexual abuse in her life and that her life was unmanageable. She believed that God could restore her to sanity. She made a decision to turn her life and her will over to the care of God. She definitely was ready to do whatever it took to break the pattern of sexual abuse in her family and her life.

Next, Rosita did a searching and fearless moral inventory of her life. With deep anguish she realized how running away from her pain and acting out of anger had affected her marriage and her children for years. She began to be more conscious of how her angry reactions to her pain had hurt a lot of other people in her life, including her abuser. She was able to admit all this sordid matter to God, to herself and to another human being through a major confession covering the whole of her life, as far back as she could remember. She experienced a great liberation from guilt, fear and anxiety through these Steps.

In the process of doing all this, Rosita became more aware of her own defects of character, which had made her act out and hurt others. She reviewed all the hurt that had come her way, all the violent actions that had been done to her, and how she had chosen to respond negatively. She saw that she had resorted to coping skills and defense mechanisms to protect herself from further hurt.

Those skills had worked in the past but were not working for her anymore. She learned that she could not live the last half of her life the way that she had lived the first half. She had to move on to deal with her defects and heal from them. She began with human insecurity, anger and resentment, false pride and stubborn self-sufficiency. She included shortcomings such as the need for control and power in her life, impatience with others, and low self-esteem.

Rosita also learned the key and core teaching of the gospel of Jesus, the need to forgive one's enemies. Her own relative had made himself her enemy, and now she was ready to move towards trying to forgive him. She had experienced the forgiveness of God for her own hurtful actions in reaction to how she had been hurt by him and others. Now she was ready to begin the process of letting go of revenge and starting to forgive those who hurt her, starting with her abuser.

Rosita began by writing a letter to her abuser, trying to practice that skill of communicating with love that Jesus taught in Matthew 18:15: "If another member of the church sins against you, go and point out the fault when the two of you are alone."

After writing many letters, sharing them with me and discarding them, she finally wrote one that she could honestly say was written with love, with no attempt at revenge or getting even. It was a pure communication of her painful feelings flowing out of the hurtful actions her abuser had inflicted on her 35 years earlier. Rosita then moved on to praying to God to heal her anger and resentment especially. She got ready to have God do so in a very incarnational way, by communicating her pain to her abuser with love as a way of letting it go.

We arranged to trick her abuser into a meeting. To his credit, he came even though he suspected that something was up. Rosita read her letter to him and cried her way through it. I was there as a support to her and also as a witness, as is described in Matthew 18:16: "But if you are not listened to, take one or two others along with you, so that every word may be confirmed by the evidence of two or three witnesses."

Her abuser responded initially by minimizing the gravity of his actions, claiming that his actions were normal for young people at that time. She held her ground, did not accept that excuse and read the letter again. This time he offered to go to the police. She replied that was not necessary. All she needed was for him to know how she felt about what he had done to her.

Then Rosita did something that we had not discussed and on which I had not coached her. She asked him to forgive her for the way she had treated him for 35 years, in reaction to the hurt that he had caused her. Both her abuser and I were shocked. I could hardly believe my ears. Then, to top it all off, she got up, went over to him and gave him a hug. I almost fell out of my chair. He then left and I was in a daze. I congratulated her on her amazing, grace-filled healing work. For her part, she was beaming with gladness, filled with joy and exulting in a new-found freedom.

I have since then seen her at a family banquet with this man, and even dancing with him at a social event. When Rosita shared this story at a retreat months later, a religious sister came up to me later and said to me, "That's impossible." She could hardly believe it. What could I say? I agreed with her that it was impossible for us, but for God, anything is possible.

Truly, Rosita had come full circle. She had experienced the pull of the gospel and had responded in faith and love. She had truly lived the words of Jesus. She had loved her enemy, had forgiven the one who abused her and had poured kindness on the one who hurt her. She had lived the gospel and was now living in the kingdom of God. In doing so, she became a source of hope for other victims of abuse. She had accomplished an impossible healing journey.

Scripture

Forgive your neighbour the wrong he has done,
and then your sins will be pardoned when you pray.
Does anyone harbour anger against another,
and expect healing from the Lord?
If one has no mercy towards one like himself,
can he then seek pardon for his own sins?
(Sirach 28:2-4)

Prayer

Lord, you alone know our hearts, our story, our original wound.
You alone can empower us to deal with that excruciating hurt,
as you dealt with your own hurt on the cross, through forgiveness.
Heal us of our anger and resentment
and fill us with the exhilarating joy and peace of genuine forgiveness
that opens the way to reconciliation. Amen.

Love Too Hot to Handle

A good friend of mine, Claude Sheehy, is an energetic, dynamic, lively French Canadian. At one time in his life, he had a lot of nervous energy that he expressed by using his hands a great deal whenever he spoke. He was tremendously loved by the people he served as an Oblate missionary. That personal uniqueness and special relationship shone in a humorous way during a conference in Thunder Bay, Ontario, many years ago.

Mary Lou Iyahtal was the master of ceremonies during the social evening. At one point, she asked Claude to come up on the stage. Once there, she had him turn around, asked him to put his hands behind his back and tied them together with a cord. Then she ordered him to turn around, face the people and talk. Claude obediently turned around, opened his mouth and stood there speechless. Not a sound came out. He could not speak because his hands were tied. The effect was hilarious.

155

Years later, something similar happened to me on October 19, 1999, during a celebration of my 25th anniversary of priesthood in my home parish in Delmas, Saskatchewan. It was an incident that since then has caused me to reflect and pray over the role of love, affirmation and expressed affection in our lives as individuals, as families and as Church.

The life lesson I learned from this incident was the importance of being able to be loved, as well as to love.

Up to that point, the anniversary was an interesting mixture of events: a mini vocations awareness tour, the release of *Northern Nuggets* (an earlier version of *Drumming from Within*), promotion of the Missionary Association of Mary Immaculate (MAMI), as well as promotion of the new Cree hymn book, which had been revised by Bro. Tom Novak OMI of Winnipeg and printed by the Archdiocese of Keewatin-The Pas.

First, I toured the northern communities of Canoe Narrows, Cole Bay, Jans Bay, Beauval, Île-à-la-Crosse and Pine House, where I had served as pastor. These former parishioners appreciated the opportunity to celebrate a 25th anniversary of priesthood locally. I was grateful for their generous hospitality and the opportunity to visit with my Oblate confrères Germain Turcotte, Nestor Silva and Joe Jacek.

Then it was off to Battleford for supper with my niece and godchild, Keltye Lavoie, and a relaxing, informal "Come and Go" afternoon and evening the next day at the Oblate residence.

On Sunday, October 24, friends, family, relatives and former parishioners joined the parish of St. Jean Baptiste de la

Salle in Delmas for the Eucharist. Celebrating with me were Fr. Leo Mann OMI, our provincial superior at the time, and former Oblate Steve Andreas, who was pastor of Saddle Lake and my Cree language mentor.

Songs in French, Cree and English, as well as a special offertory procession by nieces and nephews, added to the celebration in the church. Presentation of Mary Sisters Rita Bisson and Raymonde Arcand, with whom I ministered as a team for six years in the Battlefords area, helped with the liturgy. Viola Nicotine of Red Pheasant represented the First Nations of the area. Elder Mary Sapp, who had attended the Delmas Indian Residential School as a young girl, provided a historical connection.

A reception took place after the liturgical celebration. I had envisaged a very simple light lunch with perhaps a few comments. That was before my late brother and sister-in-law, Louis and Judy Lavoie, got involved as facilitators of the event, and the parish decided they would do it the way they do best.

On short notice, Judy organized a beautiful program. Fr. Leo spoke very affirming words as my provincial superior. Linda Hebert, who was married to my cousin Daniel the same year I was ordained, sang "Here I Am." Her rendition of that hymn stirred up some of the same feelings that it had raised at the ordination itself.

I appreciated the affirmation of friendship and cultural awareness that former Chief Harry Lafond of Muskeg Lake shared with the gathering. He had been a fellow novice with me in 1970 at the Oblate novitiate in Arnprior, Ontario. Harry was our diocesan coordinator for First Nations ministry in the diocese of Prince Albert. He had also represented the Canadian First Nations people at the Bishops Synod on the Americas.

Verna Whitford of Sweetgrass First Nations emphatically affirmed the effectiveness of our team ministry in the area and sang an introduction to a song that was rooted in her own culture and uniqueness. Verna is an accomplished Christopher instructor who has helped give the course in numerous communities. Her talk was a perfect four-step Christopher talk. She is a great entertainer and often regales people with her humour as Cajun "Queen Ida."

Steve Andreas, a former Oblate and colleague, spoke warmly of our friendship and Oblate brotherhood. Steve and I resemble each other so closely that he has at times received hugs intended for me. Though we are alike in many ways, we are also quite different. Fr. Albert Ulrich OMI probably expressed it best: "There is Steve, aiming ... aiming ... aiming ... and there is Sylvain, shooting all over the place!"

Interspersed with the speakers was the reading of telegrams from my sister Jacqueline Little in Ladysmith, BC; a family friend, Jeannette Schiller of Victoria; a cousin, Roland Lavoie of Rimouski, Quebec, who wrote for the relatives in the east; two of my nieces, Solange Nicholson of Calgary and Chantel Lavoie of Toronto, as well as greetings from Bishop Gerry Wiesner OMI of Prince George and Bishop Adam Exner OMI of Vancouver, who was my ordaining bishop.

The parish of Delmas was so gracious and hospitable. People such as Lawrence Blouin, Raymond Lacoursiere and

Jeannine Grosjean, the workers in the kitchen, and the new pastor, Fr. Frank Anuszkiewicz, made it all come together like a large family gathering.

It was such a pleasure to gather with friends and former parishioners. To name a few, Wes Jamieson and I were classmates at White Cap School in Highgate for eight years, while Ray Hudon and I attended university together. Virginia Bird, who has shared her healing journey with me over the space of many years, came from La Ronge with a friend. Former northerners, including Len and Lorraine Dupuis, Les and Liz Hurlburt, and Clem and George Hood were also present.

I am grateful to my family who were there: Louis and Judy, brother-in-law and sister Colin and Adele Turuk, brother Roger and sister Jeanne O'Quinn. I think they were all running on post-harvest energy. Having my uncles and aunts there was also very special. Aunt Antoinette Duhaime is the youngest member of my late mother's family. Uncle Louis Gregoire spoke humorously for them all, and I discovered that Auntie Thérèse is a cheerleader as well as a dancer. Greatly missed were Gerry and Aurelia Hebert, my godparents, who have both passed away.

I am so grateful for all who came. To celebrate an anniversary of priesthood is to celebrate our common baptismal commitment as well as who we are as Church, the Body of Christ. And my experience of us as Church, especially as an Oblate and as a priest, has been truly life giving and rewarding. It is my hope that young people, perhaps even some who were there, might give serious consideration to the possibility of God calling them to a similar vocation.

It struck me later that at the reception we were living out the gospel for that day: "Love God, and your neighbour as yourself." We had "loved God back" in the liturgy, and now all those gathered were truly loving others and loving me with their affirmation. I was honestly learning of my need to grow in love of self by simply accepting all that love. What a challenge that was and continues to be.

At the reception, I was moved, touched, overwhelmed, perhaps even in shock. It was difficult for me to simply receive all that love and affirmation. At a certain point, it became more than difficult; it was actually beyond me. After the cheer led by Aunt Thérèse and the strong words of praise spoken by Verna, a strange feeling came over me – a kind of disassociation, as if this had to be about somebody else. All those kind, loving, affirming, praising words were too much for my system to take in.

And when it was my turn to speak, like my friend Claude, I, too, was at a loss for words, even though my hands were not tied together. I responded with a joke, a humorous poem, and a general thank you. I couldn't touch on what everyone had said. I just could not go there. That love was, for me at that moment, too hot to handle. And even though I was very grateful for all that had been said and done, I felt sad afterwards. I thought and felt that by not responding more appropriately, I had in a way deprived the speakers of the love and affirmation they deserved in return. I regretted the loss of an opportunity for the people present to get to know the speakers and my family a little better, which would have added to the occasion.

I still struggle with that challenge. Since then I have reflected on what happened. How is it that I, a priest who preaches about love and forgiveness almost every Sunday and who taught courses on confidence and affirmation, would have so much difficulty receiving that same love, acceptance and affirmation when it was offered to me?

What a revelation for me. What an opportunity, painful as it was, for continued healing and growth. What a priceless self-awareness, which is the basis of all personal growth. What food for thought and meditation and prayer.

We know the commandment to love others, and probably try to follow that commandment to the best of our ability. But have we allowed ourselves to hear the last part of that commandment of Jesus: "as you love yourself"? How able are we to receive love? How free are we to love ourselves? How well do I love myself?

How do we as individuals, families, Church and society handle love in our lives? How often do we compliment others and how well do we accept compliments from others? How often do we affirm others and how well do we accept affirmation from others? How often do we express affection to others and how well do we receive the affection that others try to express to us?

At a deeper level, how often have we avoided developing a friendship or a relationship with someone else of either gender because of a fear of intimacy or of being talked about by those who don't understand intimate relationships and are afraid of them in their own lives? Do we realize that perhaps our cultural milieu and social conditioning deprive us and our loved ones of a life-giving experience of the gospel of Jesus Christ, who said that, above all, he calls us friends, and not servants anymore?

Was it not because he loved, and loved deeply, intimately, compassionately, that Jesus was crucified by those who could not handle that kind of love enfleshed in their own midst? Instead, they had run away from the challenge of expressing love, compassion and affection by hiding behind the smokescreen of a much safer and more proper piety and religiosity. Could it be that in our lives there is more of the scribe and Pharisee than we care to admit, but perhaps need to examine?

These are questions I have asked myself since that day in Delmas. I know that deep within each of us there is a hunger, a deep-seated desire to love and to be loved, to be free to express and receive affection, to affirm and to be affirmed.

One of the passages of the gospel that I have come to appreciate and that has moved me most profoundly is in the gospel of John, where Jesus makes a deceptive yet striking statement, that he will reveal himself to those who keep his commands (John 14:21).

The command, of course, is to love one another. It dawned on me during a retreat one day that what Jesus means is that those who love by achieving genuine intimacy and oneness, in deep trust with another human, will experience him. They will experience him because he and the Father and the Spirit are relationship, unity, oneness and, especially, intimacy. To be close to God, we must be closer to people.

Perhaps each of us can truly say that at times we have either loved or been loved in a wholesome, appropriate and healing way, and have enjoyed the mellowness and well-being flowing from that experience. That is meant to be the kingdom norm. Would that we would all, including me, dare to overcome all fear and socialized obstacles that prevent us from being truly and fully loving and alive human beings and children of a God who is love.

May we never again find our hands and our tongues tied when it comes to expressing and receiving love and affection, compassion and caring. Happy anniversary!

Scripture

"They who have my commandments and keep them are those who love me;
and those who love me will be loved by my Father,
and I will love them, and reveal myself to them."

(John 14:21)

Prayer

Lord Jesus, you wept over Jerusalem,
and over the death of your friend Lazarus whom you loved.
John, the beloved disciple, lay his head on your breast at the Last Supper.
You were at ease with the woman who washed your feet with her tears,
and dried them with her hair.
Give us the freedom to express our affection for one another,
and the ability to accept love and affection when it is offered to us. Amen.

With Jesus in Our Boat

His voice was warm and friendly, but his question, "Are you sitting down?" set me instantly on edge. His next words led to an incident that reminded me of an important lesson for life: with Jesus in our boat, we can weather any storm.

What followed that question by Peter Sutton OMI, archbishop of the Archdiocese of Keewatin-The Pas at the time, was the statement that my name was being submitted as a possible successor for him as archbishop, as he was due to retire. His next question was "Will you let your name stand?"

Needless to say, I was in shock and almost speechless. Stunned, I barely heard him say that he had special permission from the apostolic nuncio in Ottawa to inform me of this development. He added that the appointment would only be as coadjutor until his resignation was accepted. He explained that coadjutor, unlike auxiliary, meant having the right to succession.

Realizing that he was serious, I asked for some time to discern this volcanic eruption into my life as an Oblate missionary to the First Nations people in the heart of Plains Cree country. He suggested I take a week to pray over the matter and call him back.

I made my way to our Oblate cottage at Amyot Lake in northern Saskatchewan and entered into an Ignatian discernment process. I thought about this development long and hard, reflecting on its implications for me and for others, including the Oblates and the people I was serving. I then prayerfully and reflectively weighed the pros and cons of saying "yes," and the pros and cons of saying "no."

If I remember correctly, the negatives outweighed the positives. I called Archbishop Peter back a week later and shared the outcome with him. He listened patiently and discounted my reasons against, one by one. He reminded me that I would need a very serious reason to refuse, and that the Oblates also serve the Church. He ended up by telling me that he thought I was saying "yes."

Realizing that I had to give an answer one way or the other, I said that I would let my name stand, thinking as I did so that the routine investigation to follow would uphold my negative reasons and that the appointment would never come to pass.

As the months rolled by, the conviction that I had no need to worry grew stronger. After a year, I was so sure they were looking for someone else that I accepted an invitation from Fr. Alfred Groleau OMI to go to Pakistan in September for a month of ministry there. He asked me to give a retreat to the scholastics, leadership courses and addictions awareness workshops. I was looking forward to the trip.

Then, on July 3, 2005, I got a message from the apostolic nuncio on our answering machine, asking me to call him as soon as possible. He was warm and friendly, but his message caused the earth beneath my feet to shake: "Pope Benedict XVI has appointed you coadjutor archbishop of the Archdiocese of Keewatin-The Pas. Do you accept?"

Realizing that I had had over a year to refuse, I had little choice but to summon what courage I could and quietly accept. It would be announced a week later, on July 11, and was to be kept *sub secreto* until then.

The day the news broke, I was fortunate that the Oblates of our cluster had planned a get-together in Battleford, Saskatchewan, where I was surrounded by a supportive community of confrères. From that day onwards, however, it was like stepping on a fast-moving train. Archbishop Peter's first words to me after the announcement were to get to The Pas as soon as I could. We set the date of the ordination for a mere six weeks later and started the process of planning and preparing. My trip to Pakistan was the first casualty of this new commitment in my life.

There followed a quick trip to Montreal to get fitted for cassocks and to obtain the ritual gear needed by a bishop. Next was the need to bring closure to my ministry in the Loon Lake area, pack and move to The Pas.

A priority for me was a retreat. I was able to arrange four days at the Benedictine Abbey near Muenster, Saskatchewan.

There was some additional stress for me going into the retreat, as a young couple wanted and insisted on having a priest to bury the stillborn baby they were expecting. I visited them en route to the abbey, prayed with them, and left them with the assurance that Bro. Kurt Stang OMI would be there to help them.

On the way, I had a session with my spiritual director, Sr. Teresita Kambeitz OSU, in Saskatoon. She was excited about my appointment and suggested some themes to pray over during my pre-ordination retreat, including to be grateful, to listen, to stay humble, to celebrate and to enjoy. Those themes would prove to be powerfully providential.

By going on retreat, I had stopped the whirlwind of activity and had time to pray, to let this new reality sink in and to experience my emotions. The first day of the retreat, I woke up feeling a strange, inexplicable sadness. Not taking that feeling too seriously, I prayed with the first theme, gratitude, without any great insight and with some dryness. As the morning wore on, the feeling of sadness deepened and developed into a full-blown feeling of fear and anxiety bordering on depression.

Those powerful emotions fed on each other. The reality of what was about to happen was now starting to feel real. It was true. I was going to be made an archbishop, something I had never wanted and never thought would happen. This was not an obedience of three or six years. It felt like a life sentence of seventeen years until I could retire. My life was predetermined, decided, set in stone. I felt panic, fear, perhaps some anger, rebellion and worst of all, depression looming on the horizon like a black cloud.

Those dark emotions brought back memories of a time in my life 15 years earlier when a combination of burnout and depression hampered my ability to minister effectively and led to months of recovery and therapy.

The positive side of that most painful episode in my life was that I learned some hard lessons that can only be learned by suffering, by what St. John of the Cross would call the dark night of the soul.

As priceless as those lessons were, and as much as they have enriched my ministry since then, I would not wish that pain on anyone. And here, on the first day of my retreat to prepare for my ordination as an archbishop, I was feeling that same depression return. I felt a deep, fierce, penetrating fear. How could I be bishop if that same scenario was to repeat itself? Was God playing some kind of trick on me? I did not understand. I felt confused and afraid. The anxiety and depression grew stronger by the minute.

I went for a very subdued walk around the monastery grounds. I tried to avoid meeting or talking to anyone. I felt listless, despairing and not at all like praying. Finally, I forced myself to pray. I looked at the next theme, listening, and could not find any suitable passage on that theme to pray over. The only one that surfaced in my commentary was "Then pay attention to how you listen; for to those who have, more will be given; and from those who do not have, even what they seem to have will be taken away" (Luke 8:18). That was hardly a consolation.

However, as my eyes gazed down the page, I noticed just a few verses below the passage, where Jesus was in the boat with his disciples, sleeping. A storm came up and the disciples were full of fear. I immediately identified with their fear and the storm in my life that was threatening to overwhelm me. Could this be coincidence, or the work of the Holy Spirit? Believing it was the latter, I decided to pray with that passage.

As I sat there on a hard wooden bench, forcing myself to read, ponder and pray, I could feel fear and anxiety looming and depression washing over me like a wave, pushing me down and stifling my spirit.

Then I would read the words of scripture and, like a delicate breath of fresh air or a slender green shoot pushing its way through the earth, I would feel the beginnings of hope and confidence emerging.

The Bible states that the Word of God is "living and active, sharper than any two-edged sword, piercing until it divides soul from spirit, joints from marrow" (Hebrews 4:12). That was what was happening to me. Here are the words of the passage I chose to pray with:

> One day he got into a boat with his disciples, and he said to them, "Let us go across to the other side of the lake." So they put out, and while they were sailing he fell asleep. A gale swept down on the lake, and the boat was filling with water, and they were in danger. They went to him and woke him up, shouting, "Master, Master, we are

perishing!" And he woke up and rebuked the wind and the raging waves; they ceased, and there was a calm. He said to them, "Where is your faith?" They were afraid and amazed, and said to one another, "Who then is this, that he commands even the winds and the water, and they obey him?" (Lk 8:22-25)

I had never prayed with my emotions like this before in my life. The emotional storm raged within me for an hour. On the one side, waves of fear, anxiety and depression would wash over me, pressing down on my spirit and pounding away at me like the surf against the shore. Then I would read and ponder the words of that passage again and, from the other side, waves of faith and hope and confidence would wash over me, buoying me up and floating me effortlessly along. Back and forth I was tossed like a small craft in the sea. Little by little, the rudder of faith and the waves of hope began to gain the upper hand.

And suddenly, the hour of prayer was over, and there was calm. Like wisps of dark clouds banished by the wind after a storm, the feelings of fear, anxiety and depression were all slipping away or gone. In their place, like warm rays of the sun breaking through the clouds and the gentle dripping of water drops from the branches of trees after a storm, the delightful feelings of faith, hope, peace and confidence settled in.

Then other powerful, pleasant emotions asserted themselves. I felt free, liberated, relieved and full of joy. I could hardly believe it or contain myself. Could this be really true? Then it dawned on me: it was true and it was real. Jesus had just liberated me from the demons of fear, anxiety and depression, just as surely as he had quelled the storm and calmed the waters for the disciples that day on the Sea of Galilee.

I now felt humbled and grateful, which were two of the themes over which I was invited to pray. I had already experienced them in a powerful way. What had previously taken months of therapy to heal, faith in Jesus and his Word accomplished in an hour.

I knew now that this was God at work, preparing me for the storms that would await me as a bishop in the Church and the world of today. I felt ready now for whatever might come. And storms did come. Even before the retreat was over, external factors threatened to upset the preparations for the ordination, but I was ready to overcome the obstacles that presented themselves.

And so it has been to the time of this writing, almost a year later. What a spiritual gift that retreat was for me. That gift can be for all of us, if we remember that with Jesus in our boat, we can weather any storm.

Scripture

"Blessed be the Lord God of Israel,
for he has looked favourably on his people and redeemed them.
He has raised up a mighty saviour for us
in the house of his servant David, as he spoke through the mouth of his
holy prophets from of old,
that we would be saved from our enemies and from the hand of all
who hate us.
Thus he has shown the mercy promised to our ancestors,
and has remembered his holy covenant,
the oath that he swore to our ancestor Abraham,
to grant us that we, being rescued from the hands of our enemies,
might serve him without fear, in holiness and righteousness
before him all our days."

(Luke 1:68-75)

Prayer

Lord Jesus, you who calmed the storm
and called the disciples to stronger faith in you,
grant us that same faith in your presence in our lives,
free us from fear and anxiety,
and continually remind us that with you,
we can weather any storm we encounter. Amen.

Afterword

I hope that these pages have offered you an enjoyable sampling of the life of the Church in northern Saskatchewan and Manitoba over a period of 30 years. Certainly they have given me the opportunity to express the privilege I have felt in ministering within that Church.

One motive for writing about these experiences is to invite youth to consider and reflect seriously on their call or vocation within the Church to a life as a deeply committed lay person, diocesan priest, religious missionary sister, brother or priest, or even bishop. (If it could happen to me, it could happen to another unsuspecting soul, too!)

I believe that to truly realize our God-given purpose in life, each of us needs some commitment that is greater than ourselves, a commitment that will constantly challenge and stretch us. Such is the nature of a truly committed Christian life of service.

The challenges are great, but they pale in significance when measured against the rewards that come from a life of serving God's people. How can one describe the rich sense of fulfillment, the depth of meaning that pervades life when one journeys with others as individuals or as a community? How can one measure the rewards that come from helping others tap their human potential, heal their life's hurts and realize the freeing depth of God's love for them?

If these stories of faith meeting life stir in one young person the desire to serve the Lord in a more deeply committed way, then may the Lord be praised. *Haw, ekosi.*